A Collection of Thoughts

TIMOTHY HEDRICK

Cover art by Adam Hedrick

INFINITY PUBLISHING

Copyright © 2011 by Timothy Hedrick

ISBN 0-7414-6667-8

Printed in the United States of America

Published September 2011

INFINITY PUBLISHING
1094 New DeHaven Street, Suite 100
West Conshohocken, PA 19428-2713
Toll-free (877) BUY BOOK
Local Phone (610) 941-9999
Fax (610) 941-9959
Info@buybooksontheweb.com
www.buybooksontheweb.com

Table of Contents

Foreword

I was driving home through the beautiful fall landscape of southeastern Pennsylvania, thoroughly enjoying nature's beauty, when I began to kick around the idea of writing this book. I needed a working title, so I let my mind wander—*A Collection of Thoughts*—I like that. "Okay," I thought, "the book will be a grouping or collection of essays about life experiences and what we learn from them." Initially, these experiences were my experiences.

Then, after a few weeks of posting the essays on my website, my friends began to call me with essay ideas. "Hey, I just drove past this sign; it said 'Expect Delays'—that could be the title of one of your essays," a friend said.

Another friend told me about her daughter and the struggles she had reconciling her past. I said, "Why doesn't she just rearrange her past?" I wrote "Changing the Past" after our conversation ended.

This pattern continued throughout the writing of the book, right up to the last essay, "The Butterfly Tree." As Anne and I were talking about the idea of this essay, our good friend told us that watching the butterflies in her garden comforted her as she recovered from cancer.

For me, writing this book has been a wonderful journey of self-discovery and, most importantly, the discovery—and in some cases the rediscovery—of the people in my life. Aptly titled *A Collection of Thoughts* is just that.

My intention is to open up the great possibilities that life offers, to open the avenues of love, understanding, and acceptance. I know how great life can be; I feel the magic within all of us. The time has come for each of us to reach deep inside and find the person we want to be and then become that person.

Enjoy the book!

Tim

The Sun

Darkness. The earth is quiet. Like an audience awaiting the majestic notes of a brilliantly crafted symphony, the world silently anticipates the upcoming dawn. Suddenly, a solitary note, appearing as a breath of light, stretches along the horizon as an illuminated ribbon of orange and red. As radiant as the reflection of love in a new mother's eyes, the sun's glowing fire breaks the night's grasp and forms a new day. Creation.

Rising into the morning sky, the sun displays supremacy and glory, magnificence and power, grace and beauty. Effortlessly. Living nature responds to the sun's caressing rays, as the plants and flowers turn toward the source with abiding reverence. Awakening.

Ascending like a determined mountaineer, the sun climbs steadily, reaching its summit in the sky. The full strength of our marvelous sphere of heat and energy now penetrates the atmosphere, freely giving her gift of warmth, never thinking of reciprocation. Life.

Transcending energy engulfs the day; earth's inhabitants are animated with activity. The populace of our planet, in a shared relationship with this energy, is creating a day that will exist only once. Cooperation and turmoil, happiness and sadness, success and failure, dreams realized and dreams shattered, all incorporate this day. Every want, every need, is either filled or denied. Fate, never resting, casts its spell upon the unsuspecting. Destiny awaits those who dissolve fear and uncertainty, then with execution, deny fate another conquest. Love abounds, love flourishes, and love grows, although so do hate and prejudice. Possibilities.

Flowing colors illuminate the sky. Lavender, crimson, aqua, and white swirling within themselves; a grand collaboration created for us by the artists of the universe. Sinking slowly from sight, the sun exits with the splendor and brilliance produced only through the infinite potential of nature. Celebration.

Darkness. Night, a welcome time for rest and quiet reflection, is upon us. The day, now a masterpiece nearing completion, becomes yesterday, as preparation for a new day begins. Regeneration.

Back Roads

I love to drive. I especially love to drive convertibles. There is something magical about driving through the open air. The speed is enhanced; the sound of the engine is clear, and driving becomes an art form. Plus, it is **very** romantic. When I drive, I prefer to drive back roads. Sometimes, I actually do need to get to where I'm going and choose, along with the masses, the highway, but I limit these encounters to necessity. Yes, the big, fast, vast highways have the advantage of reducing distance with speed, although I think back roads have advantages, too.

Driving the back roads invigorates my mind and brings me closer to nature. Two lanes of asphalt conforming to the twists and turns of the terrain carry me to the quiet and serene regions that have a wonderful propensity for clearing my sometimes-overloaded imagination.

The natural beauty along the back roads is fantastic. Small trees and shrubs diligently try to recapture the area cleared by man, staking their claim at the edge of the road. The larger trees stand guard just beyond the scrubs, their branches laden with the leaves of summer. The trees are effortlessly beautiful and deeply rooted. Wildflowers join the mix, adding a wide scope of color; they complement the various shades of green and are perfectly placed in repeating patterns.

And nature's fragrances! The top must be down or, at the very least, the climate control off, and the windows open for full appreciation of those magnificent aromas. The sweet scent of honeysuckle and the earthy smell of the soil combined with the distinctive fragrance of sassafras root are a joy. The plants growing along the banks of a nearby stream create a most heavenly bouquet. This unique and marvelous scent is like a mysterious perfume that has been fabricated from exotic herbs and spices. The cleanliness of the air, itself odorless, acts as a catalyst for the other aromas and is refreshing and invigorating.

My favorite part of traveling the back roads is uncovering the small towns along the way, more specifically, meeting the people who live in these small towns. The inhabitants of small towns are incredibly open to my questions, and I love listening to their stories, especially when their stories are accompanied by a nice meal and a glass of wine. No one seems too bothered by the fact that just an hour or two before our impromptu get-together we were total strangers; when we meet again, we will consider ourselves friends.

Traveling the back roads is not without risk. The chance of taking a wrong turn is greatly increased, and street signs are few. And, I am very careful to avoid accidently veering into the water-runoff ditches alongside some of the back roads I travel. At times, my route is blocked by a fallen tree or a mudslide: with no alternative, I must turn back and find another way. Except for the people living in the small towns, very few people are around. If I were to run into trouble, the trouble would oblige me to use my imagination, discover the solution, and then execute it myself. My patience may be tested and my arrival delayed, but I fully accept these conditions.

The back roads are filled with endless adventures and discoveries. The next time you head out, slip past the crowded highway, find an alternative route, and experience the pleasure found driving the back roads.

The Great Wind

It all started with a slight breeze. Two hours later, the wind was a consistent fifteen to twenty miles per hour with blustering gusts. I thought this crazy weather would pass quickly, but I was wrong. The heavy wind lasted more than forty-eight hours—it disrupted outside weekend activities, caused the waters of the bays and rivers to become turbulent, and was the reason many trees lost their weaker limbs.

When the great wind finally subsided, the sky cleared and was bathed in a marvelous shade of light blue. Without clouds, the sky seemed to be born again, clear of any harmful particles, all impurities transitioned from within by the great unrelenting wind. "Nature's way of cleansing the atmosphere," I thought. Unrest followed by turmoil, then new life and calm. Nature is so perfect in her processes.

Such a weather-related event is not unlike the conditions you may experience when your life is in transition. Think about a situation when your life changed dramatically, whether it was a change in a relationship, a career change, or you making a conscious decision to change a habit or a behavior. The process begins with your thought of what can be. This phase is like a slight breeze, a mild wind of change, scarcely noticeable, although present nonetheless. The next phase is the choice to take action. The internal winds intensify, gaining momentum, and result in a rising storm of emotions and uncertainty. Within this storm are the seeds of an improved life, although not quite visible and felt only through faith; these seeds are your vision of the future. A stronger wind, now with the force of purpose and the intensity of destiny, carries away your present situation and creates the void required to fulfill your new beginning. The seed, your vision, takes root. The wind diminishes and then dissipates. Then calm. Destiny realized, a new dawn.

As you grow and move forward, your life will become full of transitions that when addressed with faith, a belief that the end result will be positive, and a pure understanding that these transitions create the knowledge required for improvement, will leave you fulfilled. Only through turmoil can you appreciate peace, only through the winds of transition can your foundation be strengthened, only through clarity can you have real vision, and only through love of self can you love others. Nature is so perfect in her processes.

The Question

"What do you want to be when you grow up?" Throughout my youth and young adulthood, I dreaded this question. I dreaded it because I didn't have a clue of what I wanted to be when I grew up or if I even wanted to grow up, whatever growing up meant. "The question" was first asked at home. Then, when I was about fourteen years old, "the question" was asked at school. What's funny is that the guidance counselors who had pressed my classmates and me to answer "the question" had also admitted that if they had been asked "the question" at age fourteen, they would not have chosen to become guidance counselors. I didn't see the point in investing any real thought in answering "the question," so with indifference I told the counselors that I wanted to be a rock star. This answer was unacceptable on every level. My counselors replied that no one makes it as a rock star, and I should take "the question" seriously and make another choice. So I answered with the next best scenario I could think of—to be rich and famous. Not one of the counselors nodded with approval. "The question" remained a part of my life for a number of years. Only after *I* asked myself "the question" did I begin to get answers.

I take nothing away from the good intentions of my parents and educators; I, too, believe in setting clear and definite career goals. That being said, I believe the more pertinent question should be this: *Who would you like to become as you grow?* Or perhaps more specifically: *What type of person would you like to be, both now and in the future?* Answering this question is advantageous since there is no need to wait to make and implement decisions; the application of the answers can begin immediately. As the emphasis is transferred from "what you are going to be" to "who you are going to become," the pathway for complete personal and professional success is revealed. For sure, only after "who" you are going to become is discovered can career choices even begin to be considered. In essence, what someone does to generate income is of little consequence within the creation of "who" he or she is. As a matter of fact, if we concentrate on the personal development of people first, aren't we preparing them to become stronger in their profession through a greater understanding of themselves?

When we introduce the thought of creating the person you want to become, we also set in motion a process that brings immediate gratification as well as a lifelong pursuit of personal growth and development. Imagine the definitiveness of who I am going to become corresponding with the dream of what I want to be. In other words, the vision of who I will become is an absolute, whereas the career decision remains variable. This separates the development of personal traits and the development of career into two distinct parcels, each a separate entity to be cultivated individually.

Appreciating Nature

I love the Travel Channel. I love seeing exotic places around the world and visualizing visiting those places myself. Outside of my television-viewing daydreams, I have been very fortunate and have visited many great places. A recent trip to the Pacific Northwest, the Oregon coast in particular, was just incredible. I really appreciate the beauty and wonder of nature, the sunrises and sunsets, the contrast in colors, the mountains, snow, and, yes, even rain. I love the feeling I have when I take the time to really see the natural greatness around me; the harmony within nature is fabulous. As much as I love this feeling, for a period of time I unconsciously reserved it for when I was away from business or when I was vacationing.

During this period of my life, I would use my morning drive to mentally prepare for the upcoming business day. And I would use my evening drive to analyze the day's events. I rarely noticed the sun rising or the season changing as I drove; I was so focused on business that I did not absorb much outside that bubble. Then something changed. As we were completing the audio CD *A Fulfilled Life,* we realized we needed artwork for the back cover. As we kicked around ideas, my thoughts drifted back to a walk in Tyler Park I had taken with a friend a few years back. It was the end of fall and winter was rolling in. During this time of year in southeastern Pennsylvania, the trees have lost all their leaves, only their bare branches are visible. I told my friend I didn't like this time of year because everything, including the trees, is so barren. She then said something I have never forgotten: "Trees without leaves are beautiful. The branches are like the hands of the earth reaching up to heaven." Remembering this conversation and my friend's insight reinvigorated my love for nature. And yes— the back cover of the CD *A Fulfilled Life* features an image of a tree without leaves, its branches like the hands of the earth reaching up to heaven.

Since then, my morning and evening drives have changed greatly. In the morning as I drive through Pennsylvania's Lehigh Valley, I admire the open fields covered in a slight fog that seems to protect the wild grasses from the morning sun. I see the cornfields and pumpkin patches along with the rolling terrain, all emitting peace and tranquility. I gaze at the evening sky brilliantly illuminated by the setting sun, the clouds providing a pure white canvas for the effortless beauty of the sun's red streaming light. I feel nothing other than awe and appreciation for the beauty these scenes provide. Quite a miracle right here in my backyard, no travel required.

The benefits I receive from my appreciation of nature are immense. When I observe nature, any unneeded thoughts are washed away. Everything is brought into perspective, and I feel a calmness I can recall at will. I feel more in tune with myself, my relationships, my work, and my future, and I also have an increased awareness toward life. Not a bad deal for spending a little time each day observing the natural works of art outside my window.

As for those exotic places featured on the Travel Channel, I still visualize myself visiting them at some point; however, right now I'm satisfied with the spectacular beauty of the Lehigh Valley.

Friends with Benefits

My childhood friend and I met when we were two years old, and for the greater part of our lives, we have remained close. From the age of two until we were about thirteen or fourteen, we were inseparable. During the summer months we would meet sometime in the morning, be called home for lunch, meet up again, be called home for dinner, meet up yet again, and then be called in for the night around eight o'clock. When school was in session, we would hang out after school and then hang out after dinner until it was time to go home. All of this may sound like a pretty typical childhood friendship except for one major detail: I am a boy and Larraine is a girl.

Larraine and I loved to play sports. Along with the other kids from the neighborhood, we would play endless games of baseball or football in the sandlot field just up the street. I would always pick Larraine for my team before I picked anyone else. This had nothing to do with our friendship; I wanted Larraine on my team because she was the best athlete, and I love to win. Larraine was better at baseball and football than most of the boys, so it seemed like having her on my team was an intelligent decision. Larraine didn't receive any special treatment because she was a girl; in baseball, she got the same pitches as the boys. Likewise, in football, she was expected to make tackles and take hits. None of us ever even thought to change the rules or make exceptions. Larraine was a player—nothing more, nothing less. We were all equal. At one point, my mother called me in and told me I had to stop playing tackle football with Larraine. I had just one question: "Why?" Mom couldn't give me a satisfactory answer, so Larraine and I kept playing. We would go behind our neighbor's house and play there, out of sight. We didn't understand why we shouldn't play together. No one could give us a valid reason, so we just continued playing. Larraine and I are very grateful to have had these athletic experiences.

I am not sure how the discussion started, but, when Larraine and I were about eleven or twelve years old, the talk between our families was that, most likely, we would someday be married. I guess we just accepted this and really thought it seemed kind of natural, so we went along with it. Then one day everything changed when someone—I forget whom—said that we could never marry each other because Larraine was Catholic and I was Protestant. Keep in mind, we were eleven or twelve years old. When Larraine and I discussed this revelation, we didn't understand why her being Catholic and me Protestant was an issue. It was irrelevant to us; we were and would always be best friends. Then, someone else said that if we lived in a different country we wouldn't be allowed to speak to each other: in fact, we would be enemies. Now, for sure, this was beyond the scope of our imaginations. This was our introduction to prejudice. Before this, the thought of judging people for anything other than how well they hit a baseball had never entered our minds. What seemed totally unrealistic to us was the thought that we would not be friends.

So what did we do? One Catholic girl and one Protestant boy blew off anything that would impede their friendship, including religious prejudice.

As the years of adolescence approached, our friendship changed along with everything else that was changing in our lives. Other girls and other guys, along with differing interests, began entering the picture. We were growing as individuals, and as a result, spent less and less time together. I suppose it is a lot to ask for a boy-girl childhood friendship to stay close throughout junior and senior high school. After high school, we seldom saw each other, although our respective parents would give us periodic updates about each other. Time passed, and one day my dad called to tell me that Larraine was moving back into the neighborhood. I was ecstatic. The thought of spending time with her again felt quite good. But, at the time, we were both married, to other people, raising children and making money, so we weren't able to make the reunion happen right away. It was in a moment of loss that I was reunited with Larraine. At my mother's funeral, I watched Larraine walk across the parking lot toward me. We hugged. A bond born so many years ago was still there, still strong and still pure. Since then we have become reacquainted. We see each other occasionally and talk about the wonderful gift we shared as childhood friends. The characteristics we developed together—discipline, drive, and the will to win—helped mold us into the adults we are today. We never did marry, each other. In fact, we have never been romantically involved with each other; we just like each other. One boy, one girl, and fifty years of history. Our version of friends with benefits!

Competition

I was beginning a new business project, assessing the prospects of a huge turnaround and terrific success, when into my office walked Erwin Trojansky, one of my greatest mentors. I began telling Erwin about my plans to crush the competition, dominate the area, and take no prisoners. Erwin listened intently, and when I finally finished talking, he said five words that would eventually change my perspective: "Tim, you have no competition." At the time, I assumed Erwin's statement indicated that he was as assured of my greatness as I was. It took a while for me to get his point.

As I continued to contemplate Erwin's no-competition statement, I thought, "What is he talking about? There's a ton of competition, and close by, as well." As time passed and I continued to reflect on what Erwin said, I finally got it. I don't have any outside competition; my only competition is within me. Once I grasped the concept, I began to comprehend the message. I didn't really need to be concerned about competing against other businesses or people as long as I stayed focused on improving me and my business. I would be neglectful if I didn't divulge the personal traits I had at the time. I was extremely competitive, hated to lose, had the strongest will to win, and could not be denied anything. This was going to be an interesting transition.

My first step was to completely ignore all other like businesses. In my mind, they didn't exist. I didn't speak about them; when someone else did, I simply tuned them out. I blocked other businesses totally from my mind. It was as if they had evaporated overnight. I knew I was undertaking the most challenging reformation of my career. To make it happen, I needed all of my energy. None of it could be wasted by focusing on competition. As I began to identify with the theory, I felt a strange sense of relief.

I started the rebuilding process by listing the areas of the business that needed to be either improved or outright changed. I envisioned the end product and vowed to never waver from that vision, and I didn't. Then I got to work on myself. I knew to reach the vision I had for the company, I had to improve myself; this is where the competition with me began. Just as important as the vision I held of the company was the new vision I held of myself, and I knew the success of this project hinged on these two visions becoming reality.

I completed a second to-do list. This time, I listed everything I needed to improve or change about myself. This exercise became an extraordinary and eye-opening experience. Amazingly, some of the characteristics to be replaced that I had listed were things I actually liked about myself. I felt comfortable with many of my traits; however, the competition was on, and I had to give the best performance of my life. Any part of me not held in my vision of me had to go.

The magic started to happen. I surrounded myself with terrific people. I shared the vision I held of the company with them, and they responded. We competed with only ourselves. At times, we saw comparisons between us and other businesses, but we merely used the information for the sole purpose of improving ourselves. As a result, my vision of the company was realized two years ahead of schedule. Most of the people who worked with me on this project have been promoted to management positions and are performing exceedingly well.

As for me, I achieved the first vision I held of myself and now I am reaching for the new and improved version. I love the competition. I still have that incredible desire to win, although now it is trained on the one thing I *can* control: me.

Forever

It is a perfect fall day in Philadelphia, Pennsylvania.
The ambient temperature is seventy-two degrees,
and the sky is clear, except for a few white fluffy
clouds. As the midday sun warms the air, one
forgets that within a few short weeks the city will be
in the grasp of a typical northeast winter. No need
to think about that now, though. The weather on this
day is just magical. Philadelphia is full of activity;
people are out and about enjoying the day and, in
one particular case, each other. A couple is walking
through Azalea Park holding hands, their two free
hands moving expressively, accentuating their
conversation. They are obviously at the beginning
stage of their relationship because they are
oblivious to the activity surrounding them; they are
in love and intensely locked into each other.

They met, quite unexpectedly, at a business
conference earlier this year and have spent the
warm summer months exploring each other.
Romance at its finest: weekends spent boating on
the Chesapeake Bay, evenings discovering the joy
of cooking and the intricacies of wine. They begin
their mornings an hour early just to spend time
listening to the wondrous music written by the
classical masters, Mozart and Mussorgsky in
particular. A lot of conversations, a lot of listening,
with precious quiet moments in between. As if
contained within every wisp of wind, the essence of
love surrounds them. The only commitment shared

by this couple consists of two rules—to always be honest with each other and no negatives.

Philadelphia's fall day is slowly slipping into darkness. The temperature is dropping, although it is still warm enough to be considered comfortable. The moon and stars illuminate the sky; their beauty and peacefulness add an enchanting stillness to the evening. Indeed, a perfect night for sharing. Dinner reservations are at eight o'clock. Arriving early, our couple relaxes easily until their table is ready. Once seated, wine is ordered, the menu is discussed, food choices are made, and the dinner order is placed. They are holding hands across the table and talking. During the flow of conversation, a single question is asked. "Can you promise me this forever?"

Softly, their hands release, as she reaches for and lifts her wineglass; just before she tastes her wine, she reveals her answer: "No." She returns the glass to the table and says, "All I can promise you is right now." Suddenly, a rare moment of uneasiness exists between them. Insightful and perceptive, she says, "I'll explain—I've never experienced anything like this—us—before. Do I want it to continue? Yes. I don't know what forever will bring; really, I don't know what tomorrow will bring." A short silence ensues as the server checks in. She continues, "All we have is today, and if you go deeper, all we have is right now, so all I can promise you is right now. And what if I promised you 'this' forever? What does that mean? Will we still change and grow? Will I, and will you, still change and grow?" The tone of her voice is full of love and caring; her face reflects the genuineness of her words. "I guess what I am trying to say is…. All right, this is how I feel. We are just too special to say 'let's do this forever' and leave it at that. Where will that take us? Do, or will, we lose focus on now, this moment, because we are committed to forever? I can't—*we can't*—take that chance. We can't waste one moment of now wondering about the promises of tomorrow."

The maitre d' appears and pours wine into the couple's half-full glasses. After a nod of appreciation, she continues, "I love you and when I say I love you it means I love you and nothing more. So in this very moment I love you."

"And I love you." Although in reality only a few minutes had passed, he felt like he hadn't spoken in quite a while.

"Once this time is gone, it's gone, and we can't get it back," she said with conviction. "I know what we have is special. Believe me, I know it. Do I want to be with you tomorrow? Yes. I just don't want us to get so busy dreaming of tomorrow that we forget to live for today."

He smiled and reached across the table, taking both her hands, softly holding them in his. "No promises of tomorrow or forever—just a promise of here and now?" He asked.

"Just here and now," she replied, squeezing his hands, her eyes radiating the love she has for him.

"Well, then. A toast to here and now," he proposed. As they touched glasses, both knew the chapters of their life together would be written one moment at a time.

Winter arrived with vengeance, the bitter cold settling in like an unwelcome visitor. The weather from November through February was harsh, pelting Philly with cold, wind, rain, and snow, sometimes all at once. March broke the coldness with some unexpected summerlike temperatures. The people of the city came back to life as the weather improved, many venturing to Philadelphia's numerous parks to revitalize themselves. A couple, very comfortable with each other, walk through Azalea Park holding hands, the winds of love swirling around them, writing the chapters of their lives, one moment at a time.

All Inclusive

My friend telephoned me recently to tell me about the wonderful experience he and his son had while attending his son's first professional hockey game. The only downside, my friend stated, was the tickets. The only ones available were the all-inclusive kind, which for him were not a good value because he could not use all of their benefits, but had to pay for them nonetheless.

The all-inclusive tickets included two seats, food, and admittance to the block party. But my friend only wanted the seats. He couldn't attend the block party because the game was scheduled on a workday. As for the food, my friend asked rhetorically, "How many hot dogs can a guy eat?" I thought about that question for a minute—at least four, maybe six, if I was hungry enough. Anyway, they had a terrific time, and their team had won. However, my friend still held fast to his belief that the all-inclusive package held little value. Let's review: they had a great time, would do it again, and did, but he still felt stung by paying for services that he did not want or could not use.

Somewhat like life, isn't it?

Suppose at an early age, you could telephone the order desk of life, place an order, and have your request integrated into your life. Perhaps you want a nice career that provides you with substantial income. You dial the 1-800 number and speak with the representative at **Place Your Life Order**. You request your career, and the representative, after briefly placing you on hold to verify inventory, returns with good news. "We do have that career in stock and available. However, the career you are inquiring about is only offered through our all-inclusive package."

Interested, you ask the representative to describe the contents of the all-inclusive package. "You will go to school for a minimum of seventeen years. During those years, you will receive little compensation and will emerge from your schooling heavily in debt. The initial stages of your career will produce meager results; you will live simply and without luxury. You will work many hours and have little personal time. You will be employed by several companies before you receive the career you are ordering. You will be dismissed from employment once; the effect on your confidence will be devastating. You will be employed by a person with whom you have little in common, and this person will cause you frequent distress. You will be on a proverbial path with many other people, some of whom will try to undermine you, and some of whom you will not like. You will read one hundred books, many of them more than once. You will encounter many obstacles along your route, some fixed and unchangeable, many self-induced requiring behavioral changes. Your faith will be tested, your determination pushed to the limit, and only through unwavering desire and self-discipline will you fulfill the prerequisites and the career you have ordered will be delivered. Are you ready to place your order?"

The first words out of your mouth are "I just wanted to order a great, high-paying job; I really don't want the all-inclusive package."

The representative replies, "I am sorry; that career is only available through the all-inclusive package." After consideration, you place your order.

Next on your list of life's desires is a wonderful and fulfilling deep-love relationship. You check the order sheet and there it is—one fantastic, deep-love relationship. The relationship has everything you want: Someone you can speak with freely, communicating your thoughts without reservation. A person you are able to share your dreams with, and through cooperative effort, fulfill those dreams. A relationship that through growth matures and develops, resulting in the individual development of both you and your love. Full of anticipation, you once again dial up **Place Your Life Order**. As before, the representative places you on hold and checks inventory. "The relationship you desire is in stock and available, however—"

You interrupt, "Let me guess. It is only available through an all-inclusive package." The representative affirms your statement. "Please describe the contents of the deep-love relationship package," you ask with some trepidation.

The representative begins: "You will experience multiple love relationships before the deep-love relationship you are ordering is delivered. On two separate occasions, the love relationships will become quite serious. Commitments will be made, and expectations will be presumed. These love relationships will flourish and you will enjoy bliss and happiness, although after a period of time the luster of these relationships will diminish. One of the relationships will be ended by you. The other person involved in this relationship will be deeply hurt; wounds will not heal quickly. You will be aware of the other's pain, and for many months you will be burdened with guilt. Eventually this person and you will be reconciled through forgiveness. Armed with the freedom that forgiving bestows, this person will find someone special and share a wonderful, deep-love relationship. The other love relationship will leave you deeply scarred and heartbroken. You will spend much time wondering why this relationship failed. During this time period you will discover yourself—you will learn to love yourself and respect yourself, and through these important discoveries, you will be enlightened and will fully possess the ability to love and respect another. You will be connected with your deep-love companion through a chance meeting. Both of you will immediately feel the love connection. Although your love connection creates a strong bond, this point of contact is just the beginning. To receive your order of a deep-love relationship, much learning is required. This learning is achieved through a willingness to grow in mind and spirit, both as a couple and as individuals. When the essence of sharing is appreciated, your order will be fulfilled, and your deep-love relationship realized." Knowing the answer, you do not ask about options, and you place the order.

Yes, life is an all-inclusive package. Too often, we get hung up on the situations in our lives that we don't quite understand. We also try in vain to figure out why a particular event is happening. In time, the answers will be given. In reality, these periods of turbulence are just part of the all-inclusive package, and they do have value. They serve as tools for personal growth and development. Appreciate the all-inclusive package; accept and move past what appear to be setbacks or obstacles. Only then, with splendor, will life fulfill your order.

Faith

Faith is often defined by its relationship to a structured religion. Although faith is an important part of many religious beliefs, faith also plays an important role in our day-to-day lives outside of religion.

Each of us possesses an inner faith: the faith we have in ourselves. This faith often dictates our actions, the way we make decisions, and the overall quality of our lives. As this inner faith grows in depth and strength, many aspects of life improve through increased self-confidence and higher self-esteem. In the course of conducting many interviews, I have found that most people lack self-esteem and self-confidence, which creates internal havoc. So how can we increase our self-esteem and confidence? How does inner faith work? And how can it grow and become stronger?

Faith and trust go hand in hand; you cannot have one without the other. Therefore, having faith in yourself is another way of saying that you trust yourself. By having faith in yourself, you trust your actions and your decisions. You eliminate self-doubt, and this faith allows you to flourish and be happy. That being said, do we always have complete faith in our decisions or actions and do we always trust ourselves? Or are we jilted by self-doubt? Truly, we all experience some self-doubt or lack of confidence from time to time, only because we fail to follow one of the oldest and most perfect methods of knowing what to do and when to do it. Nature provides us with an inner-detection device that notifies us immediately when we are on the right path and when we have strayed too far off course. This internal system is often referred to as trusting your gut, following your heart, or going with your instincts. This internal system guides us in the direction that is right for us, if we choose to use it.

There have been times in my life when I was unsure of a decision I had to make, and I incorporated the help of others. Sometimes I went against my gut feeling and followed the advice of others. This caused me to move in a direction that was against what I felt was the right path for me. I soon discovered that traveling in a direction that went against my inner instincts didn't feel good; at times, it was frustrating and often unfulfilling. At some point, I made the choice to trust my inner voice and tune out the thoughts of others; this was the beginning of what was for me an incredible transition. As I began to have faith in myself, to trust my gut and follow my heart, I set in motion *my* plan for *my* life. Since the day that I reached that realization, every aspect of my life has greatly improved. I excel at my career, my personal relationships are all I hoped they would be, and I feel fulfilled. I now have complete faith in my decisions, the direction of my life, and the choices I make. I also trust that living through my heart will yield me the most wonderful of life's rewards: happiness.

Trusting this inner faith is the greatest gift we can give ourselves. Each of us is responsible for the life we create, for the actions we take, and the results of our decisions. This is a great and wonderful task, although no simple chore. Nature understands the complexity of our task and is ready and willing to help. We only need to listen, have faith, and trust our gut.

The Critic

My grandmother was known for serving burnt cookies. Not burnt-to-a-crisp cookies, just ones that were slightly singed. My sisters and I would tease her about it all the time.

"Everyone's a critic," she'd reply. We meant no harm, nor did she take offense. In fact, I believe that she would leave the cookies in the oven a few extra minutes on purpose. One, because she really seemed to enjoy the peals of laughter elicited by her cookie-baking adventures, and two, how else could the legend of her burnt cookies have survived for decades?

In reality, Grandmom's cookies, burnt or not, were delicious. So delicious, in fact, that she had to hide them to prevent us from devouring all of them in one sitting.

I have experienced the other side of the coin: criticism cast with caustic indifference. I daresay we have become a society that is quick on the draw when it comes to pointing out the faults, failures, and weakness of others. In a never-ending search for others' deficiencies, we scour our resources until we find the desired information. Once compiled, we exhibit an insatiable longing to disclose our findings en masse while disregarding the consequences. This behavior is of no value. In fact, it creates much harm and discord.

Criticism is a double-edged sword, equipped with a blade that never dulls. I have been victimized by this sword, by both the giving and receiving edges. A general misconception about criticism is that only the receiving edge of the blade causes pain, when actually the giving edge leaves the deepest scar.

Criticism is a negative deed; this is fact and cannot be debated. It is important to understand that when we criticize, we unleash lethal emotions that burn in the souls of those involved.

Criticism diminishes the self-esteem and self-confidence of the person on the receiving end, causing him or her to emphasize the exposed fault. At times, such faults receive an exaggerated amount of relevance, and the person loses sight of one's positive qualities because of this increased focus on what are considered inadequacies. Again, the result is lack of self-worth, lowered self-confidence, and lack of self-esteem.

Giving criticism is as devastating as receiving it, the fallout masked in ignorance. Criticism is most efficient at reversing its direction; therefore, when criticism is directed outward, its tendency is to reverse course back to the initiator. During this reversal, the quantity of criticism is multiplied infinitely. In other words, when we direct criticism toward another person, we are in fact generating and directing massive amounts of criticism back toward ourselves. A cycle of negativity is generated that exists forever, unless it is modified by its source.

Simply put, to end the rampant and unnecessary evil known as criticism, each of us must take responsibility for its demise. How difficult would this be? Actually, the solution is effortless and uncomplicated: just a graceful change in vision. If we let ourselves see only the best in the people surrounding us and accept them for who they are, amazingly, we will build a rapport of respect and appreciation that will be shared, as our acceptance of others is reflected back to us. Set the example. Start to quell criticism today.

Changing the Past

Based on the vision I have of a future conversation between a dear friend and me...

I didn't like my past, so I changed it. In particular, I didn't like carrying the perceived baggage of my past. The weight I had hung on myself because of past events was like the weights and chains carried by the ghost of Marley in Dickens' *A Christmas Carol.* Every experience that had caused me pain or discomfort or just didn't turn out the way I wanted it to, I quickly converted into one more link of chain, one more lead weight. Failed love relationships, family issues, friendships gone sour, and times of loneliness and sorrow I perceived as losses and held them close, always. The burden was heavy; I felt sorry for myself. Why, I asked, should my life be this way? I was frustrated and angry. Then I made a valuable discovery. Through my fascination with biographies, I found my past was not much different from others; in fact, in many ways my life so far had been much better than others. The difference was in the way I perceived my past—more specifically, in my interpretation of the events I considered failures or losses.

I revisited my past with a much different attitude. The first step was to stop asking why. It didn't really matter why something happened; it happened and I couldn't change that. What I could change were the thoughts and feelings I had toward the events that made up my past. Instead of viewing particular events as failures or losses, I began viewing them as gains. This became possible as I started to picture my disappointments as learning processes, and through these learning processes, I found a way to break the unwanted patterns of my life. Through a wonderful awakening, I realized that the ending of a relationship, either love or friendship, was not as tragic as I had thought. In fact, it would have been more tragic if I had not had the opportunity to experience the love and friendship that existed within these relationships. Yes, in some instances I wish the relationship had continued; however, I am very grateful for the love and friendship shared and, most important, for what I learned.

I recognized the efforts of my parents, and with a sudden surge of appreciation, I realized the tremendous love they have for me. I released the negative feelings I had concerning my past. Some of those feelings still haunt me, but with persistent effort, I move forward. I have accepted my past, every part of it. I hold no grudges. I have no regrets. I have forgiven those who needed forgiveness, including myself.

I have changed my past. I no longer feel the pain I once held on to so dearly. I feel appreciation for just being me. No longer fettered by the past, I am able to construct much better todays. I am free to live for today and dream of tomorrow. The strength once required to haul the baggage of yesterday I now use to create the life I want.

Now that I am on good terms with my past, I am free to create my future and fulfill my dreams. As the darkness of my past became the light of possibilities, I realized how great tomorrow could be. Doors once closed and locked are now open to me; experiences I form in my imagination are now my reality. I am free to dream any dream, and I have faith that my dreams of today are, with absolute certainty, my experiences of tomorrow. I am strong, I am confident, and I am fulfilled. My relationships are extremely rewarding—those with my family and friends, as well as my deeper-love relationships. I accept me for who I am, and I understand that the experiences of my past have created the person I am today. And it is all good.

Generation One

While assessing the last few generations, I have perceived a behavioral pattern that quite honestly perplexes me. The antecedent generation assumes some fairly general opinions of the generation following in their footsteps. The common statements made about the upcoming generation have been fairly consistent: they are lazy; they lack a strong work ethic; they want to get paid, but they don't want to work; if they are the future, then God help us; they just don't get it. This mind-set became incredibly evident to me while I was participating in a discussion group about managing the X and Y generations. As the statements listed above were applied to the X and Y generations, I jolted to attention. The last time I heard those words used to describe a group of people, they were being said about my generation. I didn't like the accusations then, and I don't like them now. I left the discussion wondering why the gap between generations occurs and the possibilities that could flourish if the gap were diminished or, better yet, dissolved.

I have thought about the friction between generations for some time and have discussed it with many people. No one has been able to give me a solid explanation for why it exists, and many dismiss it as just a part of modern life. Never satisfied with an undefined answer and believing in the need for a solution, I developed the following perspective:

In my estimation, the leading cause for the lack of understanding between the generations is a strong belief held by the younger generation about a particular circumstance or set of circumstances that are extremely contrary to the beliefs of the antecedent generation. Two examples: One of the largest generational conflicts took place during the 1960s, especially the latter part of the decade. To set the stage, realize that during the 1960s the United States was involved in an unpopular war. Civil unrest and race riots were rampant. These, along with the assassinations of prominent political and civic leaders left the decade marred by violence, hate, and prejudice. The threat of nuclear war hung heavy, and the possible demise of the human race was controlled by two powerful governments. These conditions created fear, anxiety, and a multitude of opinions.

With the increasing availability of media outlets, the younger generation could voice its opinion on a scale never before imagined. Although television was becoming a media force, the recording studio was the most accessible outlet for expressing influential thoughts. With the popularity of rock music, record companies signed thousands of artists to recording contracts, and as the recording industry evolved, artists used the medium as a social and political sounding board. Through their lyrics, the artists reflected the thoughts and views of their generation. Their musical message was one of peace, love, understanding, brotherhood, sisterhood, a world living together as one. In my estimation they were saying, "Hey, we think there is a better way. It seems we are headed for disaster. So let's look at other options." These thoughts and the corresponding actions by the younger generation raised the rancor of their predecessors, who had been raised with strict discipline and the relentless fear of uncontained communism. Neither side could relate to the other. The term antiestablishment became prevalent; anyone past the age of thirty was not to be trusted and an air of dissent stood between the generations. It was during this period that I first heard the term generation gap. Neither side had the correct approach. I can't resist the thought of what could have been. Imagine this: Two generations united in cause, openly sharing thoughts and ideas, neither side vilifying the other, cooperatively exploring the possibilities expressed through intellectual debate and dialogue. Disappointingly, both sides were separated too deeply; a chasm forged by fear, mistrust, and lack of understanding had been created that could not be bridged. Eventually, the volatile energy on both sides dissipated, ceasing the battle, albeit without solutions. Instead, what could have been a time of enlightenment is now just a page in history. This, I believe, is the true tragedy of the 1960s.

The people of the X and Y generations have been strongly accused for their perceived lack of work ethic. I know this to be a crude generalization; I have trained and worked with many hardworking and successful people from these generations. So why the negative beliefs regarding their willingness to be productive in the workplace? Let's envision what they observed and experienced when they were developing young adults. The antecedent generation in this example are the tail-end baby boomers who, maybe unconsciously, became the trendsetters for working long hours and being success driven and materialistic. I use the term "unconsciously" because I am one of those individuals and I am not quite sure how the forty-hour workweek transcended into fifty hours, then sixty hours and above. Nor do I understand how our motto became "He who dies with the most toys wins." I won't get into the wars raged against one another while we climbed the corporate ladder.

Now place yourself in the mind of a teenager watching his or her parents try to jam the mega-hours consumed by a career, the time required to raise a family and nurture a marriage, along with a minute or two for themselves, into the meager twenty-four hours that a day provides. Now imagine his or her parents telling him the following: "This can all be yours, just follow our path and you will have everything we have."

The teenager's response: "You can have it! Yes, I want to live comfortably, and yes, I want to be independent, but I want to be able to enjoy my life, too, and I can't do that working seventy hours a week!"

So we, now the antecedent generation, don't get it, and ask, "How do you expect to be anything without working fifty or sixty hours a week?"

Again, the response is "I don't want to work that many hours." Lacking understanding, the antecedent generation labels the X and Y generations as being lazy, lacking work ethic, and wanting pay without earning it. Dissension is created, frustration builds, and once again, we have unnecessary strife between two generations.

I hold fast to the belief that improving communication between the generations could yield tremendous benefits. The first step would be to open our minds to differing opinions, thoughts, and ideas. Approaching the situation as a joint mentoring process, listening and learning from each other, would yield a festival of ideas, cultivated in the spirit of social harmony, that would raise the level of the human experience beyond imagination.

Peace Within

For as long as I can remember, the topic of world peace has been openly discussed and debated by politicians, peace activists, celebrities, and musicians. Despite the efforts of many, world peace continues to be elusive. I think that perhaps the scope of achieving world peace is a bit large for any one person or group of people to accomplish. Does this mean we just give up on peace and accept war, hate, and violence as inherent parts of human behavior? I sincerely hope not.

I wonder what could happen if a majority of us really focused on peace. Not world peace, but inner peace. Peace within ourselves. Would the positive energy created by this concentration on inner peace be strong enough to dispel hate, violence, and war? I believe, and state with full conviction, that the answer to this question is yes. I have complete faith that at some point human beings will figure this out. I can't say when, but there will come a time when all of humanity will live in peace.

For now though, let's spend a few minutes considering the only element of life we can control: ourselves. Is it possible to find peace within? Can inner peace be created or enhanced?

I believe a state of peacefulness exists in each of us, that every person has the ability to live with and expand his or her internal peace.

Is it easy to achieve this state of being? No. Would
the effort be worthwhile? Yes, it would be. I believe
the moments spent with inner peace are the purest
moments we experience. Picture yourself free from
all stress, cares, hate, despair, and envy. Picture
yourself feeling only love. Crazy? Maybe.
Impossible? No. I also believe these moments
happen too infrequently. Suppose we all set aside
just a minute of each day to develop inner peace.
Imagine waking in the morning, and before thinking
a singular thought, spending one minute being
peaceful. Maybe we could expand that one minute
in the morning to include one minute in the evening.
I wonder if through self-discipline we could build
on this inner-peace foundation and increase our
peace time to five minutes in the morning and five
minutes in the evening. Could this make a
difference? To try to find the answer, I decided to
perform an experiment. I would spend at least five
minutes, three times a day, on inner peace. I would
do this for five weeks and then analyze the results.

The findings of my experiment were astonishing.
Right from the beginning, I enjoyed the few
minutes a day I would spend free from every
perceived burden in my life. I wouldn't say the
moments were utopian, although my time away
from life's distractions sure felt good. I began to
look toward my inner-peace time with greater and
greater anticipation; I started to add a few extra
minutes to my sessions, and some days I would add
another five-minute session. After three weeks, I
felt a substantial change in my attitude. I felt more

positive and, well, more peaceful. Not much of the day-to-day stuff that only a few weeks before would cause me aggravation seemed to pull me out of my peaceful state, and when it did, I could quickly perform an attitude correction and get back on track. I wasn't living with my head in the clouds; I was finding a better way to live my life. After five weeks, I was hooked. I found that the five-minute segments work best for me, and I have settled on three or four sessions per day. Although my time frame for the experiment has lapsed, I continue to use the process every day with no intention of stopping. In addition, I found that as I became more peaceful, the people in my life, both personally and professionally, also became more peaceful.

I strongly suggest that each of you conduct this experiment for five weeks. The time passes quickly and the investment pays dividends. Who knows? We could be the people who start a trend toward personal inner peace. Then, as our inner peace grows and transcends boundaries, maybe—just maybe—there would be enough inner peace to create and establish world peace. Just a thought.

Expect Delays

Out on the open highway, convertible top down, my joy of driving a modern piece of German engineering increasing with every mile. My speed constant, I was positive I would reach my destination before the anticipated time of arrival calculated by my GPS unit. Then, it happened. Appearing seemingly out of nowhere, a sign with a bold and dreaded message: "New traffic patterns ahead. Expect delays."

The usually straight stretch of highway now turned slightly to the right. I had no option but to follow the new pattern; a three-foot-high wall of concrete blocked my usual path. Then a quick turn to the left, another wall of concrete, and a slight turn back to center. Clearly, this new pattern was not the shortest distance between two points. The slower speed resulting from these twists and turns gave me the feeling that I was losing time. I checked the GPS unit and its readout reinforced my suspicion.

Three lanes became two, and many people with like destinations now fought to merge into a suddenly prized piece of asphalt. I had to slow down even more. "I should have been there by now," I said out loud to no one, my frustration increasing. Then I saw daylight. The cattle shoot that trapped me in transcended into wide-open highway about a half mile ahead. I had to tread water only a little while longer, and then I would be back up to speed.

Although I could see the breakout point, traffic slowed again, my expected time of arrival gaining minutes by the second. I was still on course to reach my destination, but I wanted to be there *now!* Then, finally, freedom. Back up to highway speed in a flash. I obsessed about the time I had lost. Eventually I let the old blues station streaming from the satellite radio free me from my self-imposed torment. At last, I reached my destination.

My destination was a beautiful paradise—the eastern shore of Maryland's Chesapeake Bay. I felt a bit foolish about the anxiety I had caused myself en route.

Something about the sound of water splashing against the shore clears the senses and the mind. Now thinking more clearly, I began to equate my traffic-pattern experience to some of the routes I had taken to reach other destinations. Not physical ones, the "life experience" kind of destinations. I have always been good at goal setting. Goal reaching is where I sometimes cause myself undue vexation. I usually do reach my goal, although at times my reaction to new traffic patterns, actual or otherwise, differed. In some instances, I accepted the obstacle, made adjustments, and moved past it. In other instances, I would try to blast through the impediment. Although I believed that the rock-crusher method would deliver me to my goal more quickly, in retrospect this process delayed it. I needed a clearer picture of how I approached my goals; time to dedicate a few moments to self-analysis. Upon examination, I found many correlations between the goals achieved with ease and the goals requiring more effort. In both instances, I had set time lines for completion, held myself accountable for achieving the goal, and was persistent. Regarding those goals that were effortless, I thought that perhaps fewer obstacles had been thrown up at me. No, actually some of the routes to achieving the least-effort goals presented more obstacles than the laborious ones. Closer assessment revealed the real inconsistency was within me. When I struggled with a goal's destination, I did not anticipate the obstacles; as a result, I was consumed by them. This response was triggered by one major factor: because I had not properly planned for the obstacles, I lost time, which put me behind schedule. In short, I did not expect delays. Lesson learned.

The path toward every goal and every achievement will be altered by obstacles, some expected, and others, not. Understanding this is extremely important when setting completion times for goals. Plan your time line realistically, navigate your route, follow the twists and turns, recognize the obstacles, and make adjustments. You'll reach your destination with time to spare.

Love

I love the word love. I love the feeling I have when I say the word love. Some people say, and I was once a part of this group, that the English language lacks an adequate number of words to describe love. In truth, love is, well, love. There are differing depths of love, although the emotion and feeling of love remain the same. The effects of love are also consistent. I know this as a fact. Two years ago, I decided to begin an experiment using myself as the subject matter. I started by writing the following statement: **I believe that if I approach every opportunity of my life with the emotion of love in the forefront and an open mind, I will be fulfilled.** I then put the principle into practice. At first, honoring the principle on a day-to-day basis was difficult. Imagine the expression on an employee's face when I said, "I love you." How tough do you think it was to say to the driver who had just cut me off, "Hey, I love you"? These, along with the challenge of saying to myself, "I love you, Tim," had me feeling a bit uncomfortable. As time passed, the process became easier and then eventually very natural. All in all, I persevered and the results have been well worth the price paid during those awkward early moments. Here are some of my experiences.

My daily commute has changed dramatically. Once I began silently addressing my fellow drivers with the words "I love you," my drive became more enjoyable. When I need to merge into a congested section of highway, I just silently say the words "I love you" and invariably someone will slow down and wave me into traffic. Yes, I still come across the driver who is in a hurry and eager to pass. With love in the forefront, I let them go by and silently ask them to drive safely.

When my thoughts are a bit scattered and I am thinking too much about whatever, I take a break and repeat the word love approximately ten times. Because nothing is more powerful than love, my mind quickly gets back on track and my thoughts are more controlled and more productive.

Love is energy. Focusing on love limits the involvement I have with the emotions that drain energy. Therefore, the time I spend engaged with anger, frustration, hate, fear, and worry is minimized. As a result, I have more positive energy and feel more vital.

My listening skills have improved. Remember this amazing point: when I love someone, I start to listen to what he or she is saying with greater focus. Being more attentive in my listening allows me to learn more about the people I am speaking with. Listening with love heightens my desire for longer, more involved conversations. During my conversations, I ask more questions, eager to gain valuable insight into the other person. My conversations are incredibly meaningful, and I love speaking with and listening to everyone.

I was very passionate about my career. Nothing could prevent me from accomplishing the goal I had set. This process was, at times, incredibly exhausting for my staff and me. When I replaced passion for my career with love, I was amazed at how easily I reached and exceeded my goals.

Faults, weaknesses, and behaviors. These discoveries were eye opening and have most definitely changed my life. As a society, we tend to look for the faults, failures, and weaknesses within others and ourselves. Love has a way of turning this around. Feeing love softens the surface perceptions I may have of another person. I now see more of one's finer points and less of what could be regarded as weaknesses. I have discovered that when I focus on only the positive aspects of a person, my relationship with that person improves exponentially, especially if the relationship was previously filled with tension and misunderstanding.

Me. I am not perfect. I have made mistakes, and I have made poor decisions, and for a long period, I would not let myself forget it. This behavior dissipated when I began to love myself. Many times, the last person to receive my forgiveness was the person who needed it the most—me. If the adage "I am as hard on myself as I am on everyone else" ever applied to anyone, it is me. I would beat myself up pretty good for making a mistake, any mistake. But love forgives all. Once I started saying, "Tim, I love you," I began to forgive myself for not being perfect. I once prided myself on being a perfectionist; now, I pride myself on my understanding that I am a work in process. I have a lot to learn, and at times I need a good mistake, followed by forgiveness, to help me grow.

With love guiding me, my relationships have become so rewarding. Every relationship I have is a love relationship; therefore, my relationships grow and have deep meaning. I cherish them all.

The experiment continues and will be with me forever. I slip up sometimes, and when I do, I take a few seconds and say, "Love, love, love." Love always puts me back on course. Give it a try.

Manners

I am immensely grateful to every person who has taken time to teach me something. I have been very fortunate; many people in my life have had an interest in sharing information with me. One of the most important lessons I learned, I now view as a gift from my parents. As a child, my parents were most emphatic about teaching me perfect manners. Believe me, this was not an easy task; I was not always a cooperative student. However, with my parents' persistence, I eventually developed the habit of being well mannered. Although this behavior has served me well, I'm not sure that everyone understands the importance of manners.

Manners create an attitude, a way of being that must be clearly understood. One of the oldest and most proven statements in the history of mankind states, "If you wish for others to behave toward you in a particular way, you must first use this behavior toward them." Think about the way you would prefer your interactions with others to proceed. Now visualize your conversations, actions, behaviors, and overall relationships with others. Do your real interactions coincide with your preferred interactions? How do your interactions appear? Most importantly, how do they *feel*? In general, how do other people behave toward you? Are they mannerly, respectful, and polite? Are your interactions calm, controlled, and proactive, or are they charged with quick emotional responses, rudeness, and frustration? If you are anything like me, we may share the following misconception. As I evaluated my less-than-perfect interactions with others, my perception was that the other person was at fault. In actuality, this perception was far from reality. An interaction with another person can only deteriorate to frustration if both parties contribute equally to this outcome. If one person in the interaction is polite and mannerly, given time, the other person will reciprocate. The following is an anecdote illustrating this fact: While working in customer service, my coworker developed a severe case of laryngitis; he was so afflicted his voice was barely audible. Under normal circumstances, he would have gone home to recover. However, because of a snafu in vacation scheduling, he and I were the only workers available, and the job, for sure, was not a one-man deal. So he endured and came to work determined to contribute.

Our jobs required heavy face-to-face verbal communication with our customers. Some of the customers were very frustrated with the product we serviced and were not shy about showing it. My colleague's condition required the customers to listen intently and to be patient, and they did this without complaint. At the end of the first day, we realized that although my colleague was severely limited, not one customer had been bothered by it, and in fact, the day had progressed rather smoothly. Into day two and now my colleague's voice was softer than the quietest whisper. All at once, I understood what was happening. The customers were speaking back to him in voices just as soft as his. They were following his lead. He and I discussed this revelation, and we decided to keep our voices soft even after the laryngitis had passed. We found that when we kept our voices soft and behaved mannerly, in most cases, customers reacted similarly. True story. The way others behave toward you is a direct reflection of how you behave toward them.

A greater benefit of treating others with respect and politeness is the feeling it creates within you. I can't think of a more complete feeling of satisfaction with myself as when I fill my interactions, especially the difficult ones, with kindness and appreciation. Also, I know that my act of kindness toward another will likely be passed on to at least one more person. A chain reaction of thoughtfulness is put in motion by the simple act of being mannerly.

We all share this world; we have no other place to live, at least for now. I know we can't control the whole earth, but we can control our individual piece of it. Let's polish up our manners and show everyone what a little kindness can do.

Hard Work

Throughout my life, I have heard the expression "Hard work always pays off," and for a long period, I accepted this statement as fact. I know differently now: I am currently of the opposite opinion. I believe that hard work does not pay off. I have worked very hard during certain portions of my career. As I look back on the hard-work intervals, it was during these phases that I seemed to be without direction, habitually going in circles. I was mostly tired, physically and mentally, and frustrated by how little I was achieving or, perhaps better put, how little I was earning. Not satisfied using only myself for this hypothesis, I brought my twenty years of experience as a business manager and employee coach into the equation. During these years, I observed many people who worked hard. My observations indicated that the hardest-working people, in most cases, attained the most-meager results. When counseling them about their poor results, the response was consistent: "I don't know why my performance is low, but I do know that I am working hard." They were also tired, frustrated, and going in circles. Therefore, my conclusion: Hard work does not pay off. The question: If hard work does not pay off, then what does?

The answer: The only work or effort that does pay off is work or effort applied in tandem with distinct and mindful purpose. To begin with, a channel creating reasonable expectations must be in place before there is a chance of your efforts reaping the desired results. In other words, you must have a plan. The most important part of the plan is determining the outcome *you* expect from *your* effort. Whatever this is—money, gratitude, well-being, fame, or fortune—it must be clear, and you must believe the outcome or goal is achievable. Focus on your goal often: early in the morning, periodically during the day, and before you fall asleep at night. Really focus on the achievement of your goal. Visualize the goal being achieved, see it as completed, feel the feeling you will feel when you accomplish your goal. It is also imperative that you have faith in yourself and believe in your capability to reach your goal. When you have a clear picture of the end result, your work will develop a strong purpose, and this, in combination with effort, persistence, and desire, will pay off.

In addition to working with a plan and with purpose, I recommend working productively. I define this as creating the greatest potential for return by wisely using your greatest investment, time, with directed effort. To determine your level of productivity, track the amount of time spent performing the tasks that move you closer to your goal against the predetermined amount of time you set aside for work. You will find this to be a fascinating study. After a week of tracking your actions, along with the time used to complete them, you will be amazed by the additional available time you discover.

Another application of time management is to use time segmentation. Segment your day into blocks of time, then assign meaningful tasks within these blocks. Remember to schedule breaks from work and use break time as wisely as the time you spend working. A quick change of environment during your break is incredibly beneficial; if possible, take a walk outside during your time away from work. Also, keep in mind the objective of a work break is to refresh your mind and body.

Working without direction and purpose is hard work, and hard work is just hard work, nothing more. Although I now work with a direct purpose in mind, I still, at times, become a bit tired. The difference between being tired during my hard-work period and being tired in my current circumstance of purposeful work is well stated in a quote from one of my colleagues. After a very successful day, during which he achieved all he had proposed to achieve, Del said to me, "Tim, I am tired, but it is a good tired."

Work with purpose, play with purpose, plan with purpose, love with purpose. They all pay off and reward you, every time.

The Garden

Living in the Philadelphia area has a lot of advantages. One benefit I appreciate in particular is the Philadelphia International Flower Show, held each spring. Impeccable gardens, carefully manicured, fill the convention center with their incredible beauty. Roses in full bloom, their color as deep as the finest red wine, their fragrance is just as intoxicating. Rows of perfectly placed tulips, in multiple colors, appear like a rainbow that has fallen to earth. The rich soil, the mosses moist and luscious, and water features flowing over well-placed rocks, all set in precise harmony, inspire my soul. I value the talent and commitment of the horticulturists and the gardeners. To me their skill for creating with nature rivals that of the old masters applying paint to canvas.

Along with manmade gardens, I have a deep affection for gardens created purely by nature, untouched, unimpeded upon by any force other than the whimsical wishes of the Creator. I especially love the gardens that seem to be very wild and out of control. These gardens are full of shrubs and grasses with multiple varieties of wildflowers, all components intertwined in an effortless quest for magnificence. One of the best examples of this form of garden was visible from a road I travel daily. I would slow the car as I neared the garden, taking a moment to admire its beauty. I would do this every day. And then one day, the unthinkable happened.

The garden had been cut down to just aboveground level. My heart ached as I drove by. I drove in silence for an hour, devastated by the loss of my garden.

Not being one to allow a negative experience to overwhelm me, however, I searched for the positive aspects of the garden being cut down. I changed my thought from the garden being cut down to the garden being harvested. Thinking of the garden being harvested allowed me to believe and feel as though the flowers and shrubs had been taken for a good reason. I realized that during the harvest the seeds of the garden's flowers, shrubs, and other assorted plants had been loosened and released to the wind. They are now traveling to another location, and with the guidance of nature's hand will begin another garden. Many of the seeds fell directly to the garden's fertile soil, which now has greater access to the providers of life, the sun and rain. I thought of the wonderful opportunity I have of observing the garden being reborn: the realistic prospect of the new garden developing and becoming even more intense and beautiful than the original. I know that the space created by the harvest gives the garden room to grow and expand its possibilities. As I passed the garden the next morning, I did so with a new perspective and new appreciation for the wonderful potential the garden embraces as it becomes renewed.

For me, a perceived loss is now a realistic gain—not an ending, but a beginning. New growth and endless possibilities. What could be better?

Unique

I visited the Classmates website of an old friend of mine. Her answer to the question, "What type of person were you in high school?" consisted of just one word: "unique." A perfect self-description. This caught my attention for a couple of reasons: first, because she *is* unique, and second, because the first sentence from the epilogue in my book *A Fulfilled Life* is "I believe everyone is unique, with differing special talents and abilities."

I do believe this statement is true. I also believe that at times our uniqueness is sometimes restrained or placed in the background of our lives. It takes a bit of courage to allow our uniqueness to be out in the open, to share our most outrageous thoughts, and crazy dreams. I wonder how many of these thoughts and dreams go undeveloped because we don't have the courage to share or pursue them. Furthermore, how many inventions, discoveries, and advancements would not have happened if the person who had that outrageous thought or crazy dream lacked the courage to follow through?

As I was conducting the research for *A Fulfilled Life,* I studied a lot of people who had achieved great success. Many of them shared common experiences. The most common one, however, was that many of them had been ridiculed and criticized when they made their intentions public. Bringing their ideas from the dream stage to reality took strong desire, persistence, and the ability to block the negative input from others. These great people are, without doubt, unique.

At some point in our lives each of us has had a thought or idea that if cultivated could have brought us success. In most cases, these thoughts never moved past the point of being a daydream or past the development stage. The most common cause for this reaction is fear. We fear what others will think and what they will say. We fear being criticized. What a shame. The desire and focus of the great people I encountered during my research were deep enough and strong enough to allow them to move past the negative thoughts of others. For most of us, however, this would be a daunting task.

The tag line of my company, Sun Ray Group, is "Improving the world, one person at a time." That one person begins with me. I work on myself and share what I have learned with the people enrolled in our classes and seminars and through my articles and books. An area that I improved within myself is my appreciation of everyone's uniqueness. This includes their outrageous ideas and their crazy dreams. In fact, since I've taken this new direction, I find more and more people are sharing their ideas and dreams with me. I love the expression on a person's face when I give my support and communicate what a great idea he or she has. I know that sometimes just a little encouragement or direction will spark the person into action; a few words of support transpire into confidence, and suddenly, a wispy dream becomes reality.

The fire of individuality and uniqueness burns in us all. Ambition, dreams, thoughts, and ideas are bursting beneath the surface, waiting to be cultivated. Visualize this: Opening up your idea and dream bank, then sharing these thoughts with people who will support and help you further your ideas, you subsequently turn the process around as you support and encourage their ideas. Keep that scenario in mind the next time someone honors you by sharing with you personal dreams or crazy ideas.

We all are unique. We all have distinctive thoughts, varying perspectives and aspects about our personalities, which, when combined, create our individuality. The more we accept and appreciate one another, the more we can accomplish. Through others' thoughts and dreams, we expand our thoughts and dreams, and open each other up to endless insight and possibilities.

He Said, She Said

He said, "Who are you?"

She said, "You know who I am."

He said, "I know your name, but I don't know who you are."

She said, "I am an angel. I'm here to show you how great life can be."

He said, "An angel?"

She said, "Yes, an angel."

He said, "Well, my life is good. I'm happy."

She said, "I don't think you're being honest with yourself. I think there is something missing."

He said, "Okay, life could be better. I mean, yeah, I could be happier. You have to take what you get, right?"

She said, "Can I ask you a personal question?"

He said, "I suppose so; go ahead."

She said, "If you had one wish, one thing in life that mattered most to you, what would it be?"

He said, "...I would love to have the feeling I have when I first fall in love with someone, every day. You know that feeling? When you first realize that the other person loves you and you love them, like the sun and its rays are radiating inside you."

She said, "I know the feeling."

He said, "Nothing else seems to matter. I can go days without sleep and not be tired. Miss meals and not be hungry. Work is great. With her, even those infernal knickknack shops are tolerable."

She said, "It's magical, isn't it? So why do you think you can't have that feeling every day?"

He said, "It just never lasts very long. One day you wake up and you're back to normal life. The trash needs to go out, the lawn hasn't been cut in three weeks, the job really is a drag, and you find out being in love is a short-term remedy."

She said, "I believe anyone can have that 'in love' feeling every day."

He said, "Maybe in your angelic universe."

She said, "I don't like sarcasm."

He said, "Sorry."

She said, "Don't say sorry. No apologies. I am just telling you how I feel. If I shared my thoughts on love with you, would you be okay with that?"

He said, "Sure. Please."

She said, "Okay. A lot of us hold true to the belief that the 'in love' feeling is created when someone loves us. We wait until that person shows up in our life to be in love, although what is really happening is we have become infatuated with being loved. This is not being in love. This is being loved. A nice feeling, although being in love is more. It is deeper, it is very special, and it starts from inside. To be in love with someone else, you must first be in love with you. That feeling of having the sun radiating through you that you want so much can be yours every minute of every day when you are in love with you. Only after you are in love with you first, can you share love and be in love with someone else."

He said, "That seems self-serving, to love myself."

She said, "Exactly! You are taking care of yourself first. You're starting to get this!"

He said, "Do you love you?"

She said, "Yes, I do love me. I accept me as me. This is who I am and I'm okay with being me. I'm not perfect, nor do I wish to be. If I were, I couldn't grow. By accepting me and loving me for who I am, I can accept and love others for who they are."

He said, "You are special."

She said, "I'm just me; that's it."

He said, "I thought you were an angel."

She said, "...I am."

You Can't Care More

During the course of an employee evaluation, Delbert said, "You can care, but you can't care more." The employee we were discussing was a person we believed in, who had all the tools. However, despite excellent training and our efforts to motivate, the employee continued to underperform. I was dismayed at my inability to guide this person to that aha moment—the moment when someone gets it, when everything comes together and one's potential is reached. I thought that I must have been missing something.

"You can care, but you can't care more."

At the time, I believed wasted talent and ability were a crime, a hideous offense, and I believed myself to be the cure-all for a person falling into that category. Many times, I succeeded. But when I didn't, the lack of results haunted me. "You can care, but you can't care more."

Delbert was telling me it's okay, it's all right, we did our best, they did their best, we can all move on now. But I refused to accept the fact that I could not get this person to perform. I just couldn't lose; I felt I had to find a way to coax everyone to his or her maximum potential.

"You care too much."

"You can't care more than they do," Delbert's follow-up sentence hit home. I understood his point, although I didn't know how to change.

I knew Delbert was speaking from experience. A few months prior, I had noticed a change in his behavior. His usual charming and easygoing personality seemed just a little off. The effortless laughter was there, all right, but without its usual conviction. At first, I thought little of the change; after all, we were winding down what had been an exhausting year. Del was just tired; it would pass, right? It didn't.

Then, Del's work performance faltered. Not by a great margin, but enough to cause concern. He assured me everything was okay. But I knew him well enough to see past the words and into the man, and knew that everything was not okay.

Del always listened to anyone who was going through a rough patch in life. He not only listened, but he also became involved. He would offer advice and follow through; the other person's problem became his.

A few days passed and we spoke again. This time, Del opened up. He told me that so many people were calling on him for advice and help, he was feeling overwhelmed. He was not overwhelmed by the number of requests. On the contrary, he was troubled by the lack of improvement exhibited by the people he was trying to help. This weighed heavily on him. Del had overcome many struggles himself and was committed to helping others pick themselves up and get back in the game. But it wasn't working. Then he realized the effort he was putting forth was greater than the effort that they were producing.

Del was caring too much. He made a strong decision. He told each person who had sought his counsel but were not working toward a solution to stop calling him unless they were willing to play an active part in remedying their problem. The next day, Del was back to normal. "You can care, but you can't care more."

We can all learn a lot from Del's experience. As managers, coaches, parents, and teachers, we all want the best for the people we train, teach, guide, and rear. Why? Because we care. As I reflected on not caring more, I wondered how this was going to work out. Could I care less? No. I thought about what Del had told his help-seekers: "When you are willing to be involved with the solution to the problem, call me." He wasn't going to fix their problem for them; the solution had to be a joint effort, or he would not be involved. The answer for me was not caring less; the caring had to be equal on both sides. At times, when training or teaching, the situation can become an us-against-them mentality. You will learn, you will perform, you will behave this way. I will not listen, I will do it my way. And so on. These exchanges occur subconsciously. Although the intention is to get the message across, a gap in communications occurs. A gap that needs to be eliminated.

I began to view training and teaching as a sales process. I reviewed the basics of selling: present the product, list the benefits, overcome objections, and close the sale. I would present my product, information, and knowledge; go over the benefits; hear the concerns or objections; overcome them, and close the sale. To me, the closed sale is the person on the receiving side accepting the fact that we are working together toward a common goal with a cooperative plan in place to reach that goal. This is not always a quick process. I know I have to be patient; most of my time is spent overcoming objections. However, the more I persist, the better the overall results. An unwanted change in the process is easily corrected by reminding people of the benefits they are suddenly not receiving.

Students, employees, anyone receiving advice, training, or information from a teacher, employer, or parent, always remember the benefits you are receiving. Foremost, the people sharing the information with you are doing so because they care; they believe the information being shared is advantageous to you. This is a gift. Others are taking a genuine interest in your development, sharing their knowledge and experience with one purpose in mind—to help you create a better future. Be open to and cooperate with the people in your life who are helping you create a strong future. You will not always agree. There will be concerns and objections. Work through them as a team and create the future you desire.

As the caring scale is leveled, extraordinary results begin forming. It is amazing to experience what transpires when two or more minds work toward a mutual goal.

Taking Inventory

I once worked in a retail store, and on one night of
the year, every year, my coworkers and I had to
physically count the store's entire stock of
merchandise. Inventory Night. What an enormous
task it was. Every item had to be counted, from
items on display to items in the stockroom. As if
that undertaking wasn't big enough, after one of us
had counted the merchandise once, another one of
us had to count it again. I strongly disliked
Inventory Night.

I believe that we feel the same way about taking
stock of ourselves. Some faithfully perform the
dreaded task once a year, usually around January 1.
Others do a surface inventory or simply bypass the
Big Inventory altogether.

But lack of commitment to self-inventory and self-
examination sentences us to a life lacking the
fulfillment we could so easily have. I imagine most
of us begin our day with an exterior inventory. We
check our appearance in the mirror before we set
out. But, how often do we check our inner
workings, our sub and substance? Many of us rarely
study our core. Why?

Taking personal inventory is a task that few of us
perform. If we look closely at ourselves, we see our
strengths. But, we also see our weaknesses. Honest
assessment is difficult. Not many of us really want

to delve into the dimensions of our personalities that need to be changed. Sometimes these qualities are so deeply rooted that opening them requires a concentrated effort. This is where self-analysis can get interesting—and become very rewarding.

The best technique for self-inventory or -analysis is to complete a self-analysis evaluation. One of the best is in Napoleon Hill's book *Think and Grow Rich*. Hill covers all the bases. When you complete this evaluation, you have a clear idea of what makes you tick.

Completing the evaluation is just the beginning. Creating a list of the characteristics you want to improve, and addressing these characteristics, builds a more complete you. The rewards are fantastic; shedding yourself of unnecessary and unproductive traits or habits reveals many possibilities that were previously either uncultivated or unseen. Release yourself from the tethers holding you from achieving your goals, and set sail for a truly fulfilling life. Take inventory of yourself today.

Trees

I love trees. Some of the best times of my life have involved trees in one way or another. The property where my parents' house is located is surrounded by acres of woods. "The woods," as my young friends and I called them, were our refuge, our real-life jungle gym, and our sanctuary. We climbed the trees, we swung from them, just like Tarzan, and we built forts in them. We forged paths through the woods, and as we got older, the paths became trails for our motor bikes. The trail system we built was so vast; we were able to ride all over town without leaving the woods.

The woods became quite memorable for Larraine, my most special childhood friend, and me. As we explored the woods, we found secluded creeks and fields of wildflowers and skunk cabbage. We found a unique area of undergrowth and declared it to be our own place. We swore to never tell anyone else about it nor show it to anyone else. We would hang out in our place for hours, planning the future, or just talking and eventually, in our place, we would share our first kiss. To this day, whenever I visit my hometown, I never leave without walking through the woods.

My grandfather was a master carpenter. He designed, constructed, and had installed the kitchen cabinets in our family home. He was a genius craftsman who built the cabinets with love and appreciation for his materials. The doors of the maple cabinets were edged in mahogany. The cabinets themselves were unstained, allowing the wood's natural beauty to subtly shine through several layers of varnish. I remember watching my grandfather recreate spindles for antique furniture to replace the damaged originals. His replications were perfect. The wood responded to his hands like magic, and the finished products showed his love for his craft. I truly believe that the trees my grandfather appropriated for his projects are pleased with the results.

I love the tranquil splendor of a forest during a snowstorm. I love to admire the snow collecting on the evergreens, their needle-filled branches effortlessly bearing the snow's weight and showcasing the beautiful frozen crystals.

The artist's palette, with its endless combinations of color, requires every skill its master can muster to reproduce, on canvas, the extraordinary landscape that the trees offer as they prepare for winter. Yes, the leaves are going to fall from the branches; however, before the leaves and branches part company, nature gathers its imagination and creativity for one fantastic organic fireworks show. Thank you, trees.

Trees are a tremendous source of inspiration. Their roots travel deeply into the soul of the earth, forever seeking the nutrients required for their growth. These subterranean branches anchor the trees with magnificent strength, supplying an unseen foundation, determined in purpose and unwavering in execution. The tree trunk, mighty yet flexible enough to withstand nature's fury, allowing it to bend though rarely break, displays a steadfast will to survive. The tree branches forever reach upward, grasping the sky. They seem both spiritual and spirited—like nature's hands tickling the heavens.

I love trees!

Perception

The most dangerous expression I know of is "perception is reality." I find the danger of this expression especially true when it is applied toward people. No matter the perception a person has toward another, I can, with certainty, state that the perception is largely incorrect. Yet most of us carry our perceptions of others with a rock-solid belief that they are true. I believe that perceptions are only surface examinations of another person. I equate holding fast to them to floating face up on the ocean's surface—never seeing, acknowledging, or exploring its depth.

A good friend of mine was asked to be the executor for the estate of a terminally ill cancer patient. She quickly and graciously accepted, willing to do anything to help the man's family. Knowing nothing of the responsibilities or processes of being an executor, she wisely sought the advice of a person who did. This person was happy to help, and together they prepared my friend for her task, methodically reviewing the obligations of the executor. After they finished, my friend's guide cautioned her that she would learn unexpected information about the dying man, some of which she might not want to know. She was further cautioned that her perceptions of the man would, without a doubt, change. Could she handle that? Undaunted, my friend pursued her executor responsibilities with her usual unwavering commitment. She did learn everything about the man's life. And quite a few pieces of his life's puzzle did surprise her.

When my friend shared this anecdote with me, I realized how little of an individual's life any of us really knows. My friend now saw the deceased's life more fully; seeing the complete package allowed her to see who he really was, without perceptions.

We all have been told about the importance of making a great first impression. In fact, when two people meet for the first time, both of them spend approximately three seconds assessing each other. During these three seconds, a very strong perception is made, and it is so strong that it is rarely overturned. How ludicrous that in just three seconds we decide whether we like a person and determine whether an advantage exists in continuing the conversation. In three seconds. Right. Imagine the missed opportunities of this process. Oh, and the arrogance. How many times have we sacrificed what could have been a great friendship, a productive work relationship, or a mutually rewarding romantic interlude because of a perception made in three seconds?

To me, the most disturbing fact about perceptions is that they tend to be judgmental. Judgmental. Not a word that rings with harmony and understanding, or with love and acceptance. Perceptions and judgments do not build relationships. They tear them apart or prevent them altogether. Only when we look to someone with an open mind and a pure heart can we see the true colors within. The depth of the universe is within each of us, waiting and wanting to be seen and appreciated. Let's open the doors to each other and share what is real, not what is perceived.

Rain

The sun will not make an appearance today. The gunpowder-gray sky and the accumulating puddles of rain reinforce this statement. The storm of the previous evening has afflicted upon me another inconvenience, the lack of electricity. No lights, no stove, no heat, no computer, no radio, and no television. I sit on the front porch. Thankfully, it is enclosed. It's just me, myself, and I. Nothing much to do. I light a candle; okay, that's done. I pour a glass of wine. Hmm...it's only nine a.m. Let me rethink that one. I check the weather. It's still raining. I might as well get comfortable; I'm in for a day of wasted time, with me on one side of the windowpane and the dismal weather, laughing at my expense, for sure, on the other. Oh, relax. This could be fun. Yeah, right. I read a couple of pages. The candle is dim and my eyes burn from the strain. I set the book down. Resigned to my melancholy mood, I pull on a heavy sweatshirt and settle into the recliner. Silence, except for the incessant rain, creates a vacuum in my environment, adding one more dimension to my misery. I close my eyes, and, somewhat sheepishly, I find myself listening attentively to the rain.

The rain, steady and even, reverberates like a small creek flowing through a stand of woods. Without effort, the beautiful water of the creek flows steadfast over rocks and fallen tree limbs, displaying athletic grace and elegant simplicity. The sinuous course of the creek, along with the descending terrain, quickens the pace of the water, creating a harmonious aqua symphony. Gaining intensity, the creek tumbles over a cliff, free-falling onto the valley floor. Silent as it falls, the water crescendos into a thunder when it reaches the rocks. Passing beneath the mist and fog formed by water and rock colliding, the creek meanders through a tranquil meadow. Far removed from its source, the creek integrates with a small pond; the water is quiet and peaceful.

Now I hear...nothing. I check the weather. The rain has stopped. Spears of light slice the granite clouds, like a laser. Suddenly, sunshine and electrical power reappear.

Television and e-mail are back in my life. Time for that glass of wine.

Marking Time

I began playing musical instruments when I was in the fourth grade. I played in orchestras, concert bands, rock bands, and quartets, and I was a soloist during a piano recital. When I reached high school, I quickly discovered that none of this experience had prepared me for the newest chapter of my musical life—marching band. Although the ability to play an instrument remained important, a new dimension had been added: marching. No big deal, right? Not exactly. The degree of emphasis placed on the marching itself startled and perplexed me. As it turns out, so much emphasis was placed on marching, that in addition to the musical director, there were—*three*—supplemental instructors. Their sole responsibility was teaching the band to march. This was how I spent the latter part of my summer vacation—learning to march at band camp. I learned all the terms and slogans associated with marching. Dress right dress, at ease, the ever-popular attention, etcetera. I learned to march forward, to stay in step, and to correct myself when I stepped out of step. I learned how to about-face, to turn right, to turn left, and to march in predetermined patterns. I endured those hot August nights and learned to march and play well enough to become a member of my high-school marching band.

But there remained one facet of marching that I didn't quite understand—marking time. When the band marked time, it still marched, but did not move from its spot. To my dismay, the drill instructor was more passionate about marking time than any other aspect of marching. He would constantly remind us to get our knees up high while we were marking time. I remember thinking that marking time was more exhausting than marching forward, and since we basically remained in one place, why didn't we simply stand there? I knew that my opinion mattered little, so for three years I marched forward, stood at ease, and stood at attention, and, more often than I liked, I marked time.

I thought I had expunged my memories of marking time. A recent reunion with a friend of mine, however, brought those memories flooding back. Not because we knew each other during high school—we didn't—but for more compelling reasons.

My friend and I met at a local restaurant, and after a few pleasantries, we began in earnest to catch up, sharing the life experiences that had occurred during our years apart. Not long after our conversation started, I began to feel a bit uneasy. This struck me as odd, and at first, I didn't understand why. Initially, I shrugged off the uneasy feeling. After all, we hadn't seen each other in about ten years. Then, it hit me. Despite the fact that ten years had passed since we last spoke, I felt as if I was speaking with a replication of my friend as he was ten years prior. His manner of speaking, his thought processes, his traits and characteristics pretty much mirrored the person he was ten years ago. A sudden analogy shot into my mind: my friend had been marking time for ten years! Wow. I was now listening intently to my friend speak; I wasn't getting much of a chance to speak, so listening seemed the only viable alternative. I listened as my friend talked about his job changes, the lack of progress in his career, his lack of opportunities to grow professionally, and his belief that he was underpaid. Next, I listened as he spoke of his relationships—more train wrecks, one after the other. Only the names changed; the stories and results remained the same. Then the topper: I listened as he told me of the goals he had thought of setting. And then, one by one, with great conviction and detail, he explained his reasons for never trying to achieve his goals. Not only had he spent ten years marking time, but also he was working hard at it!

This account of my reunion with my friend is not intended to criticize or diminish him. The truth is, he is one of the most wonderful people I have ever known and I love him, for sure. My purpose in sharing this account is to illustrate the importance of self-evaluation. The days that make up our lives pass quickly, and just as quickly, it seems, they become months and years. At some point, we evaluate our life, and sometimes we recognize what might have been. I call this the big what-if. The big what-if can be prevented with daily self-analysis. The self-analysis process that I use is as follows:

As I relax each evening before sleep, I give myself a solid review. I evaluate my actions and my behaviors. I do this to ascertain whether they were directed toward the achievement of my goals. I also evaluate my plans and adjust them as needed. This procedure keeps me in tune with my progress and prevents me from drifting too far from the path that will lead me to the accomplishment of my goals, my ultimate destination. If you find yourself stuck in neutral, marking time and burning up energy, kick up your self-analysis process, and soon you will be marching forward, every step bringing you closer to achieving your goals.

The Boss

"You're not the boss of me!" I can still hear my little sister's screeching words, as I tried in vain to get her to do something I wanted her to do. *You're not the boss of me.* What a great statement, because in reality is anyone actually the boss of someone else?

This is an interesting question, especially for those of us who at some point in our professional careers have been the boss. To answer this question, I believe we need to begin with a clear definition of what a boss is, then perhaps we can determine who the boss truly is. The most widespread application of the boss is in relation to employment. What follows is a common picture of how this scenario functions. To become employed, one must spend time being interviewed by the boss, impress the boss enough to be considered for employment, and then, if the boss is sufficiently impressed, you, with the boss, reach an agreement of employment.

After employment begins, the boss becomes the taskmaster, holding the employee to the agreement reached during the hiring process. Within the workplace are many types of bosses, each type using varying methods to obtain their objectives. As a point of reference, I will use my vision of a great boss.

A great boss has many qualities. A boss who is firm watches over you every minute of every day, ready to correct any misstep. Sometimes strict, sometimes inconspicuous, but never faltering in the important assignment of keeping you out of harm's way.

A boss who is distinguished has a burning desire for you to live in abundance, for you to never lack or want.

A boss who is appreciative expects you to live in appreciation. Not in appreciation of him or her, but in appreciation of all the opportunities life offers you—in appreciation of your relationships and in appreciation of the natural world surrounding you. The boss who is appreciative will hold you accountable and will never accept anything other than your best effort.

The boss who is unconditional cannot perceive failure, lack of success, or complacency. The boss who is unconditional understands you are a one-of-a-kind individual, with unique traits and characteristics, and accepts you as you are.

Together, these bosses equal a great boss—a boss who cares. The boss who cares can always be relied upon to help provide you with means to cover your basic needs. The boss who cares nurtures you, helps you develop your skills, and tracks your growth. The boss who cares has a vision of the person you can become and has complete faith that you have the aptitude, the skills, and the ability to fulfill that vision. Above all, the boss who cares wishes for you to live in fulfillment and maximum happiness—nothing more, nothing less.

So, where do we find a boss like this? Good news, if we answered our initial question correctly. To my amazement, my little sister was right when she told me that I wasn't the boss of her. No, I am not the boss of her, nor is anyone else. We are the bosses of ourselves only. We may reach agreements of employment with others, but the results of employment are each individual's responsibility, no one else's. The manager is responsible for providing you with the opportunity; you, however, are the boss.

Once you accept the fact that you are indeed the boss and in control of every aspect of your life, you need to decide what type of boss you will be. Will you be lenient, accepting less than your best? Will you be critical and chastise your every mistake? Or will you be caring, taking full responsibility for your present and future, and in the process creating the life you want? Regardless of the path you choose, remember that you are the boss. The results from your efforts are yours and yours only. Embrace the task, be a great boss, and shout to the world, "YOU'RE NOT THE BOSS OF ME!"

Thanksgiving—Every Day

Although giving thanks has become a daily ritual for me, every Thanksgiving Day, I spend a little extra time thinking about everything for which I am grateful.

I am very grateful for the gift of my life. I love every minute of my life, I cherish the people in my life, and I am thankful for all the experiences life has brought to me. I appreciate the opportunities to create success and happiness, to imagine and dream big, and then see those dreams become reality. However, the one aspect of my life for which I am primarily grateful is the wonderful ability to experience love.

The emotion of love is pure, bonding, and harmonious. The inside cover of my journal bears a statement I read every day: I believe if I approach every opportunity of my life with the emotion of love in the forefront and an open mind, I will be fulfilled. Applying this theory has greatly enhanced my life. For example, it is impossible for me to criticize another person when love is in the forefront. I can listen intently to the thoughts and opinions of others, allowing them to think and express themselves freely. I can look for the qualities within another that may help me improve myself and fill me with knowledge that would have otherwise passed me by. I can respect all others through love, and this respect and love will be reciprocated to me in multiples. It is impossible for me to be discouraged when I am guided by love. Love is the basis of faith, and through faith, all of the great rewards of life are created. It is impossible for me to be consumed by negativity when I partner with love; in fact, love effortlessly repels negativity. As easily as grass grows and rivers flow, love repels—no, love dissolves negativity. It is impossible for me to suffer from fear with love in control. Love is unable to comprehend fear; love is courageous and strong.

Love allows me to see with untainted vision the reality of every situation. Through love's consent, I am able to share the most intimate and wonderful experiences only a pure love relationship can produce. Love frees me from prejudice and ill thinking; love opens the door to understanding and cooperation. Love never tires or becomes complacent. Love always prevails. Love cannot be destroyed; all love lives forever.

I believe that if I approach every opportunity of my life with the emotion of love in the forefront and an open mind, I will be fulfilled. I am very thankful for the ability to experience love.

With gratitude and love, my life is full and complete. Be thankful. Make every day Thanksgiving Day. I love you all.

It's about ME

I was in my early twenties when the 1970s came to a close. Shortly thereafter, the 1970s became known as the "ME" decade. When the term "ME" was adopted, it seemed to have a negative connotation; previous generations found this newfound freedom of "SELF" disconcerting. We the people of the 1970s were putting ourselves first.

As I remember, this change in personal philosophy was viewed as not one of social progress, but of self-indulgence. I can't even begin to understand the complex underlying social issues that drove us to become more interested in "ME." However, I do believe putting "ME" first has some very positive implications.

Putting "ME" first does not imply that others are less important: putting "ME" first represents a keen interest in personal development, fulfillment, and happiness. Many of the authors who gave us new-age thinking tell us that the path to a productive life begins with "I." Knowing and understanding "I" creates a oneness with self that correlates with a deeper awareness of one's environment and relationships. Therefore, a profound knowledge of self, gained through introspection, creates a comprehensive and well-rounded "I" that benefits "ALL." Furthermore, the advantages of placing a priority on "ME" are equal to "I" and "ALL." In other words, every gain in personal development created by "I" is received as an equal advantage by "ALL."

The following scenario is an example of a healthy focus on "ME" and the benefits received by "I" and "ALL."

To experience and share a great love, it is imperative for this love to begin with love of self. Without a focus on self-love, love cannot be shared with another. Self-love and self-acceptance provide the foundation for all love relationships. To expect another to accept and love me without equal self-love and -acceptance is unrealistic. Through self-love, I nurture my mind and seek and absorb knowledge. I take in all manners of knowledge and wisdom; I have become intellectually inspired by the great teachers of the ages. I use this knowledge to stimulate self-growth; then, just as the teachers preceding me, I share this knowledge with others so they too may experience inner growth. I allow only thoughts that are of personal benefit to enter my mind. Thus, thoughts of despair and self-doubt are denied access. My thoughts, therefore, create a mental environment of well-being and balance: others sense this and are drawn to me for advice and guidance. Through love of self, I care for my body. I respect and appreciate my body as it carries me on this path called life. The care I give my body is rewarded by perfect health; those who require my services can depend on me as a result of this perfect health. Through self-love, I feed my spirit with meditation. In return, my spirit answers for me, through the solar plexus, the deepest questions of my life. My spirit also is a storeroom for love. My spirit shares this love with everyone I meet; it passes the warm light of love from my heart into the hearts of others. Could there be a greater motive for love of self than an increased ability to share love?

I don't view placing a vested interest in creating a more fulfilled "ME" as looking out for number one; I see it as looking out for number one-half. The other half is my physical and spiritual environment (nature—the universe) and the people to whom I am connected. By way of self-love, self-appreciation, and self-discovery, I find the finest principle for loving, appreciating, and discovering others. "ME" becomes "WE."

The Spirit of Relationship

Every relationship creates an invisible energy; this energy is the spirit of the relationship. This spirit is the life of the relationship and defines the activity within the relationship. The stronger the relationship, the denser its energy this cultivates deep emotions and a dense spirit of relationship. Conversely, superficial or surface relationships contain a low level of energy, reducing their spiritual field and emotional impact as well as their significance. Acknowledging and understanding the spirit of the relationship is paramount to the success of all relationships. A strong foundation that supports the building blocks of personal and professional fulfillment is attained through an acute awareness and analysis of the energy created by our relationships. Simply put: without the understanding of what is contained inside the spirit of the relationship, we cannot productively affect the quality of the relationship.

Since all personal and professional successes are directly related to the quality of our relationships, the practice of improving the attributes of our relationships is a great benefit. How often do we take the time to look inside our relationships, to their spirit, and make a conscious effort to advance their evolution? What gains could be made if we committed ourselves to improving just one of our relationships? Let's imagine.

The work environment involves many diverse personalities. This, along with the competitive nature of many careers, creates an unpredictable atmosphere that cultivates tenuous relationships. Left unattended, these relationships can quickly become unproductive, advancing to volatile and caustic ones if left unchecked. To illustrate how damaging these relationships can be and how easy the solution is, we will use the following example. Our mock-up relationship has, because of a simple misunderstanding, deteriorated from a cordial relationship into one exhibiting uncooperativeness and strained communication. Present within the spirit of this relationship are mistrust, frustration, fear, contempt, and envy. To say this is an unproductive work relationship would be an understatement! The negative energy produced by this relationship is evident throughout the company; the negative spirit of this relationship is so strong its reverberations are being felt in the executive offices. With concern, the relationship has been discussed by upper management because of the corollary effects it is having on the staff's ability to conduct day-to-day business. Fortunately, one individual within the relationship realizes the negative spirit of the relationship is harming her performance and is also diminishing her opportunity for career advancement. Immediately, the simple misunderstanding that has sent this relationship into its current abyss is of little consequence. Knowing her career is about to take the same path as the relationship, the employee decides to take positive action.

A truly wonderful fact about this condition is that only one of the individuals involved needs to be aware of the harmful relationship characteristics. Become familiar with this fact: when one of the relationship's participants changes his or her contributing dynamics, the spirit of the relationship will transform.

The employee in our example makes a determined effort to affect the spirit of the relationship by changing her mental image of the other individual. Knowing the spirit of the relationship was once productive, she creates a mental picture that corresponds with the conditions that existed within the relationship prior to the misunderstanding. Holding this mental image firmly causes her to change her behavior toward the other person. Before long, the spirit of the relationship is back to even and is no longer a negative factor in the lives of the participants or the company.

Unchecked, this relationship had the potential to be career changing for one or both of the people involved. The advantages of nurturing the spirit in every relationship is immense; periodically, check the spirit of your relationships and, if needed, clear the negatives, then watch the magic begin.

Turn the Page

I love the New Year holiday. My love for this holiday is in part due to the traditional food and drink of the day: pork, sauerkraut, and champagne. I love all three. Although I love the food and drink associated with the New Year holiday, I also love the prospect of a new beginning. I liken the turning of the calendar from December to January to baseball's spring training. All stats are reset to zero, everyone is equal, and the rebirth of the grass on the field reminds me of nature's ability to revitalize itself. Optimism prevails; everyone is a contender.

As the New Year begins, many of us decide to begin a new chapter in our lives. We want to fill the fresh, clean, empty pages with wonderful achievements. Our goals are revitalized, and we commit wholeheartedly to achieving them. Or do we? Are we writing new pages or just rewriting the pages of the past? I believe that the following describes the typical process of creating and implementing a New Year's resolution.

To determine our resolution, or resolutions, we take inventory of ourselves, and then identify the parts that we want to improve or change. Then, we take action. At first, we are enthusiastic about improving ourselves and are dedicated to the outcome. We go at it full throttle. However, before long, our old habits creep in and we fall back to situation normal. Progress halts and we remain unchanged. Before we know it, the next New Year is upon us and we begin the process all over again. The fresh, clean pages become filled with the same old story.

How can we break this pattern? Here's how:

Unlike in baseball, we are not required to wait until spring to start fresh. We are also not required to wait for the calendar to change from one year to the next to plan our path for improvement. We can literally turn the page and begin writing a fresh chapter whenever we want. However, if we really need an event to motivate us, to cultivate our imaginations, we could use the changing of the months as an activation point. Think about this: twelve times a year you choose one improvement point and work on it for the entire month. Then, as the current month closes and the next month begins, you move on to your next goal. Every thirty days would be like the start of spring training or the beginning of a new year—a fresh resolution once a month. Combine this with the advantage of a preset time line, and you have a potent goal-achieving combination.

Keeping a journal to track your achievements is helpful. Picture how great it will be to review your journal at the end of the year and note your progress. As you fill the pages of your journal, you write the story of your life—the goals you accomplished, the challenges you overcame, and the thoughts you had along the way. Month after month, year after year, you are creating the person you have envisioned. Nothing is more rewarding.

Celebrate the New Year, celebrate life, and most importantly, celebrate with love.

The Storm

My grandfather unwittingly began a love affair that has stayed with me for the past forty years. I remember the day it all began so very clearly. One day, my parents told my sisters and me that we were going to visit our grandparents that coming Saturday morning, and that a big surprise awaited us there. Saturday soon arrived, and we all piled into the family car for the twenty-minute ride to my grandparents' house. Dad parked the Chevy and asked us to sit tight until our grandmother had greeted us. After what seemed like an eternity but was probably just a minute or two, grand mom appeared, and my sisters and I leapt out of the car to greet her. Grand mom then began to lead us to the rear of the driveway, and asked us to close our eyes as we took the last few steps toward the garage. "Okay, you can open your eyes now," said grand mom. I opened my eyes and gazed in awe. My grandfather had bought a boat! For sure, the boat was nothing remarkable. Twelve feet of aluminum and a small outboard engine. But, to me, it was the greatest boat in the world.

Over the next few years, my grandfather and I would spend many hours in that boat. We had wonderful adventures exploring many bodies of water, from the creeks and rivers of Pennsylvania to the lakes and ponds of Maine. When I say I loved the boat and being on the water, I mean I *really* loved the boat and being on the water. My grandfather felt the same way. So, it was only natural that when I could afford to, I would own a boat. And so it began. My first boat was a fourteen-foot bow rider. The next one, a twenty-one footer with a small cabin. The next one, a twenty-five footer with a larger cabin, then a thirty-two footer with lots of room. And now, a thirty-nine footer equipped with more creature comforts than my home!

These days I choose to enjoy my boat on the Sassafras River, which is located just off the northern Chesapeake Bay in the beautiful State of Maryland. The bay and tributary rivers were created as the ice caps from the last ice age melted. The water produced by the melting ice caps flowed with vengeance down what is now the Susquehanna River. The power of the water surging down the raging Susquehanna was tremendous; as the force of the water cut through Maryland's soft claylike soil, it created some of the most astonishing natural beauty. The Sassafras River is blessed with abundant picturesque scenes, from the mouth of the river at the Chesapeake Bay to the end of its navigable waters just beyond the quaint village of Georgetown, Maryland. The Sassafras River has many anchorages and coves; however, I am very fond of one cove in particular. Located just opposite the buoy marker at Ordinary Point is a small cove named Turner's Creek. Upon entering Turner's Creek, directly off the bow, there is a large cliff that is an excellent example of the erosion that took place as the bay and rivers were created. Trees, their roots exposed, stand precariously close to the cliff's edge. At the water line, fallen trees, their roots unearthed, prove that erosion never sleeps. Passing the cliff to starboard is a community dock with a large building that appears to be vacant, although at some point it must have been used as a warehouse for the watermen of the bay. Past the dock, Turner's Creek opens up and becomes a very nice anchorage, inhabited mostly by sailboats. I motor to my favorite spot in the cove and promptly drop and set the anchor. Turner's Creek is tranquility personified. The water is dead calm, lily pads abound, fish come to the surface in search of a quick snack, and it is quiet. Well, it was until the storm hit.

I was enjoying a rare and therefore very much appreciated midday nap on a fairly typical Sunday at Turner's Creek. I was resting comfortably until I was jolted from my snooze by what I thought was something striking the side of the boat. I climbed on deck and I couldn't believe what I saw. The weather had shifted, and the usually calm water of Turner's Creek was swimming with whitecaps. The wind was blowing with what felt like hurricane force, and the clouds were gray and black and very intimidating. Earlier in the day, I had removed the cockpit's camper canvas; now needing its protection, I struggled to get it in place. Every snap and zipper was a challenge, as I desperately raced against the impending torrent of rain. I watched as the cover on a nearby boat was shredded within seconds; I saw the captains of the sailboats off my port bow labor to secure their sails. Finally, with the canvas in place, and safely protected from the elements, I sat back and enjoyed nature's snarling mood swing. A perfect time for reflection.

As I watched the rain, heard the wind, felt the thunder, and was blinded by the searing lightning, I thought, "This storm seems a lot like what is going on inside me." You see, I am constantly evolving, always searching for greater understanding, seeking more knowledge, and working toward developing a clearer picture of who I am. At times, this path of discovery causes a bit of turmoil in my life. The way I see it, without spending a portion of my life in turmoil or transition, I cannot move forward. That being said, I will also say that the time spent in transition can be, well, uncomfortable.

Change is what most of us try to avoid, typically because we do not want to get involved with the nasty storm called transition. But, I love being there. The bigger the storm, the better. I know if there is a storm brewing inside me, I am transcending, I am changing, I am growing, and I am creating. Plus, I know the gains I receive from riding the storm out will be well worth the time I spend feeling a bit unsettled.

It is important to understand that whenever we set goals or visualize a better life for ourselves, and then take action to reach these new plateaus, we will spend time in transition. In a typical scenario, we begin to take action, we make early progress, and everything is fine. The waters are calm.

Unfortunately, when the wind picks up, the whitecaps appear, the rain hammers down, we run for cover. Too often, we find comfort in the past, slipping right back to where we started. This is tragic. Too many of us fail to move forward in our careers, in our understanding of self, and in our relationships, because we lack the courage to ride out the storm created by transition. I assure you that if you hang in there and brave the elements, you will survive. You will persevere and your life will be better because you looked the storm in the eye and laughed, and laughed big. I know this because I have experienced it. And, it also correlates with nature. After the storm diminishes, the winds recede and the rain becomes a drizzle. What happens next? Immense calm, peace, tranquility, and quiet. Life takes exactly the same path. After an internal storm, you will experience calm, peace, tranquility, and a new beginning. Please do not retreat from the storm. Embrace it and learn from it. Your life on the other side will be phenomenal.

As the storm passed, my internal storm subsided as well. Within the calmness of my storm's wake, I formed some resolutions that brought lucidity to my vision of the future. As I raised the anchor in preparation for the trip back to Georgetown, the captain of one of the nearby sailboats, who, soaking wet, clearly had taken the brunt of the storm, turned to me and said with a smile, "Good little blow, wasn't it?"

Indeed, a good little blow.

The Dream

One night in the not too distant past, I was in a deep
and soulful sleep. I had been physically active
during the day, and I was now rewarding my body
with quality rest. My mind was quiet—at least my
conscious mind. My thoughts were still, and I slept
in absolute peace. Without warning, I was aroused
from my sleep. Once awake I had this eerie feeling
someone was there with me. Although I saw no one,
I sensed the existence of some sort of being. Out of
the darkness, I heard someone speak. I instinctively
knew this was the voice of my unseen guest.
Through this soft and gentle voice, I was instructed
to follow. Intrigued, I moved as directed.

We found ourselves in a small room that, although
devoid of windows, was flooded by natural light,
which flowed in every direction. Deep, rich
mahogany covered the walls, which made the room
resemble the captain's quarters of a ship. On the far
wall was a fireplace. The firebox, now dormant,
was constructed of red brick and framed by
rectangular white tiles. The tiles along the upper
edge were stained brown, the remnants of an
aggressively tended fire. The mantel was strongly
built from stone. At first glance, the stones
constructing the mantel seemed to be placed
randomly, but upon closer inspection it was evident
the stones had been placed with care by the mason's
loving hands. The slate tile floor added depth to the
room. The flat-gray color of the slate was separated

by ribbons of once-white mortar that had darkened from the effects of use and time. Two high-backed leather chairs faced each other in the center of the room; the well-cared-for brown leather was soft and supple. Both of the chairs had a side table. The tables were made from cherry wood, their tops dressed with dark leather. Both tables held a crystal glass expressly designed for the enjoyment of fine wine. The setting was elegant and charming. I felt instantly comfortable in this room, and sensed that I had been there before.

From here on, I will refer to my companion as the presence, because I cannot think of a more apt description. The presence offered me one of the chairs as she, apparently, settled into the other. A fire began to burn in the fireplace. Not a raging one, my specialty, but a controlled fire that added just the right amount of warmth to the room. The crystal glasses, previously empty, were now filled with red wine, deep in color and representing well the origin of its fruit, South America. I could not make out with distinction the form of the presence. Only the voice, clearly female, somewhat indicated her identity. We tasted the wine, which was extraordinary, and we began to speak. The presence questioned me deliberately, attentively listening to my answers, absorbing my words with patience and love. She wanted to know what my future looked like through my eyes, through my imagination. We spoke of my work. She didn't call it a job or career, just my work. Interesting. She told me she could feel the desire I had to reach my destiny, to fulfill my work. We spoke of love, the many aspects of love from friendship to deep love, loving through the spirit and through prayer and meditation. We spoke of the expectations I held for my life, what gave me joy, what distracted me, what frustrated me, the creative link, and my at-will connection with that link. And, yes, we spoke about the rewards of my work. She wanted to be very certain I understood the meaning of wealth.

Her final question: reflecting on all you want from life, which experiences are most important to you? I answered without hesitation. Seemingly satisfied with my answer, she was silent for a few moments and directed me to the fire. She instructed me to focus on the fire with full concentration. As I did, I began to see a vision of my life within the flames. Everything we spoke about was there in full effect and in complete detail. Nothing was missing. The presence told me this could be my life. However, there was one stipulation. No matter what occurred, no matter how little I understood, I had to believe and have faith that the events within the flames would become real. Without delay, I agreed.

The alarm clock began playing Mozart, a clear indication it was time to awaken, and awaken I did. I felt as I had never felt before. My thoughts were clear, my intentions direct, and my faith complete. The images within the flames were now seared in my mind. I didn't know how I would bring these images to life, although that was of no consequence; I believed these were the real images of my life.

At first, I found it strange, as bits and pieces of my vision began to fall into place; then I just, well, I just expected it to happen. The more I just expected it to happen, the more it happened. Not all of my visions have become reality. Some will take time and patience. Some will take persistence. I do believe that all of them will become reality.

The dream, I suppose it was a dream, has added clarity and purpose to my life. I have direction. I know precisely what I want and, more importantly, I am clear on who I want to be. Sometimes I lose my way, although a gaze into the fire quickly gets me back on track. Remember to dream, and when you dream, know exactly what you want from your dreams. Tonight, it could be your turn!

The New Harvest

We are living in a new era. In this new era, we have
become a society that is no longer a self-sufficient
culture. In the not-too-distant past, farmers made up
the majority of our population. Each farm was a
self-contained entity that cultivated crops, raised
livestock, and without much support from outside
its fences, supplied its inhabitants with life's basic
needs. In our culture today, however, not many of
us are able to grow crops or raise livestock. So we
created an alternate means of obtaining life's
necessities: the supermarket. Of course, to acquire
life's provisions, we require something our
ancestors had less of a need for—money. Although
most of us no longer raise livestock or cultivate and
harvest crops, in our era there is a new crop and a
new harvest—again, money.

It is no secret that money is an important entity of
our society. We need money to purchase food,
clothes, cars, entertainment, healthcare, etcetera.
With so many demands on our incomes, many of us
struggle to make ends meet. However, I am of the
mind-set that with a little change in perspective, we
could improve our financial situations. I believe that
if we dig deeply into our heritage as farmers and
examine the processes our ancestors used to take the
seed from its slight beginning to the point of harvest
and applied these processes to earning money, the
results would be phenomenal.

The farming process:

Before the farmer plants the seeds of his crop, he
must first prepare. The first step is cultivating the
soil; this begins with turning the soil over by
plowing the fields. After the soil has been turned
over, the nutrients of the soil require enhancing; this
is completed by adding fertilizer. I will not describe
the ingredients used in the fertilizer; however, I
have driven past the farmlands of Pennsylvania in
the spring, and I would bet that adding fertilizer is
not the farmer's favorite part of the process! Next,
the seeds are planted, placed in perfect rows, with
equal distance between them, each seed deposited
with care and purpose. Once planted, the daily ritual
of nurturing the seeds begins; this requires much
effort and long hours of work. Although this work is
mundane and repetitive, if it is not completed the
seed will not germinate and will be denied the
opportunity to achieve harvest. The nurturing
process lasts for varying amounts of time depending
on the crop, although on average this time of
nurturing lasts between three and six months.
During this period, weeds are pulled, the soil is
watered, the progress of the seeds' growth is
monitored, and more fertilizer is added. While this
is occurring, the farmer receives nothing in
exchange for his effort. The plants are not ready to
produce a harvest; therefore, at this point, the
farmer is not receiving any compensation. The
farmer is performing these tasks with complete faith
that his work will pay off. The growing of crops
cannot be rushed. There are no shortcuts, no ways

to speed up the process. The farmer must be patient and wait for his rewards. After months of diligent work, the time for harvest arrives. The crop is harvested; a thankful celebration ensues, followed by a slight interval of rest for both farmer and field. Slight because empty fields are non-profitable fields. The process of preparing the soil must begin anew.

Okay, so how does this correlate to creating income? The processes are incredibly similar.

Earning money:

Before you can think about receiving one dollar of income, you must begin the preparation process. In essence, you are preparing for your career, and this must be completed with purpose and direction. During this phase, you will be receiving an education, gaining life experiences, and cultivating yourself for the future. This time of development is crucial. Any lack of effort, any time spent being unproductive or resistant to self-development will lessen and delay earning potential. Yes, there will be events and circumstances that will test your motivation; however, just as the farmer needs to get past the fertilization process, you must persevere and move past undesirable tasks. Once the seed of knowledge has been planted, it is your obligation to feed and nourish the seed; this is accomplished by reading something of value every day. Books are an endless supply of valuable information on every subject imaginable; you will benefit greatly by getting into the habit of reading daily. Unlike the farmer, you will not see the results of your efforts in a time frame of months; the time frame will be measured in years. Long stretches of time will accumulate without the rewards you would expect from hard work. This is okay. In this phase, you are like the farmer performing the daily ritual of nurturing the crop; it is essential that you have faith and believe that the effort you are putting forth will pay off. A very important segment of your development is your entry into the work environment. Too often, expectations of entry-level income are a bit off the charts, and you can become somewhat disillusioned when your income is less than anticipated. At this point, you are adding a second dose of fertilizer to the field. You may be required to work for less income than you perceive you are worth; however, during this period it becomes very advantageous to be open to the opportunities that are being presented. Just as the field is empty after the seed has been planted, this phase is a beginning for you and you must continually prepare for the upcoming harvest. In fact, the way you respond to events in the early period of your work life sets the tone for your career. It is important to remember that the harvest is continually cultivated by your actions; through diligence, perseverance, and effort, the harvest will grow. This process, just like the growing of crops, cannot be rushed. You must be patient, have faith, and believe. With persistence, the big harvest will arrive. After the big harvest is realized, celebrate! Then get ready to plant the field again.

The Butterfly Tree

"Look at that!"

As my eyes follow the hand providing direction, I see the most wonderful sight. Just off the grocery store's parking lot a small tree, more like a shrub, is covered with butterflies.

"That's a butterfly tree."

"I wonder what type of bush or tree it really is."

"I think it's just called a butterfly tree."

The butterfly bush is actually a summer lilac and many horticulturists use this glorious bush for the sole purpose of attracting butterflies into their garden. The stalks or branches of the summer lilac begin as a central cluster and separate as they rise from the ground. Tan in color at the base, the branches become darker at the tips. Small, green leaves start to appear approximately three feet from the bottom of the branch. The leaves become denser and larger as they continue along the branch, extending to the tip. Reaching eight feet in length, the branches bend slightly, like willows, because of the weight of the large and beautiful lilac flowers. The flowers look like a collection of small trumpets, their flared bells gathered in crowded bunches; these floral clusters are six to eight inches long and are light lavender in color. The nectar produced by the flower is honey scented; this scent becomes accentuated by the midday sun and is quite addictive to butterflies.

"A butterfly landed on your hat!"

On this day, the sun is bright and the addictive nature of the summer lilac's nectar is in full effect; there are butterflies everywhere. The yellow wings of the butterflies are edged in black with two more black lines running lengthwise atop their wings, visually separating the wings into thirds. The butterflies are either sitting on or hovering around the lilac flowers; the constant movement of the butterflies' wings adds a golden halo effect to the bush. Glistening in the sunlight, the lavender of the flowers and the yellow of the butterflies' wings gives the butterfly tree a jewel-like appearance— beautiful, elegant, and stunning—nature's pristine brilliance on display.

"Amazing what happens when a caterpillar comes out of its cocoon."

Just a few weeks prior to today's performance, the butterfly, as a caterpillar, made and then encased itself inside a cocoon. Unable to fly and lacking the beauty it now has, the caterpillar spent time in the cocoon maturing. Patiently awaiting its transformation into adult form, the caterpillar stays the course, allows nature to execute a miracle, and then reemerges into the world. After its rebirth, the caterpillar is more versatile, has more abilities, has found its true beauty, and now, as a butterfly, takes flight and celebrates a new life.

"Kind of like you and me—us—isn't it?"

"Yes, kind of like us."

Preview from *Reflections*

Author and Sun Ray Group's CEO Timothy
Hedrick shares the following three poems taken
from his upcoming book, entitled *Reflections*.

Love Letter

Precious lover, I long to be at home
With you spending quiet moments alone
My hands finding those special places
Within the warmth of our intimate embraces

Precious lover, my heart aches for you
And the special way you pull me through
You give my life meaning and direction
I give you my everlasting affection

Precious lover, I feel your love
Raining down on me from heaven above
You, as an angel, are with me tonight
Taking me through the darkness into the light

Precious lover, your spirit is near
Your voice calls me sweet and clear
Our spirits dance on romantic winds
We become one as forever begins.

The Church

I needed some quiet time alone
The separation between God and I had grown
Although I was still guided by His light
Our shared vision was gone from sight

I walked the streets without direction
Hoping and praying for a reconnection
I lifted my head and was happy to see
A most glorious building in front of me

I walked the twelve steps up to the door
I suddenly felt like I had been there before
I opened the door and walked inside
The church was so beautiful, I kneeled down and
cried

I asked for answers, I wanted God to explain
"Why has your guidance caused me such pain?"
"I am not the source of the pain you are feeling
Your lack of faith is what has you reeling"

I walked down the aisle and sat in a pew
I relaxed then prayed for a minute or two
Waves of love made me smile and laugh
I knew God was acting on my behalf

I walked to the door and started to leave
Being reacquainted with all I believe
I felt there was something I needed to do
Facing the altar, I whispered, "Thank You!"

Where Does Beauty Live?

Is beauty alive in a field of vibrant wildflowers?
Their colors illuminated by the brilliant midday sun
Is beauty found in the majestic mountains?
As they touch heaven with their snowcapped peaks

Will I find beauty in my lover's body?
Sensuous as she moves, soft to the touch
A child's smile and laugh, aren't they beautiful?
Children share joy unconditionally, innocently

A perfect melody, haunting but beautiful?
I listen to the notes believing they are a gift from
God
Monet's landscapes, are they where beauty lives?
As he magically blends color with genius

Do I discover beauty within the poet's words?
As images and emotions spill from the pages
Beauty is reflected in a love song's lyric, isn't it?
Touchingly romantic, inspiring, and pure

Does beauty live in what I see?
Is beauty alive in what I hear?
Is beauty found in what I touch?
No, beauty does not live within sight, sound, or
touch

Beauty lives in my heart, beauty is LOVE!

Only through love do I see color and contrast
Only through love do I hear God's melodies

Only through love do words inspire me
Only through love will I find the beauty within my
lover
Only through love will I be fully alive
Only through love will I be fulfilled

Beauty is alive in ME!